GAMES CRIMINALS PLAY

GAMES
CRIMINALS
PLAY

How You Can Profit By Knowing Them

Bud Allen
and
Diana Bosta

RAE JOHN PUBLISHERS
Sacramento, California

GAMES CRIMINALS PLAY: How You Can Profit by
Knowing Them. First Edition.

First Printing: February 1981
Thirty-Ninth Printing: March 2017

Cover: Design by John Bosta
        Art work by Kelly Hadveck

Copyright © 1981 by Bud Allen and Diana Bosta
Published by Rae John Publishers,
PMB 105
1390 N. McDowell Blvd, Ste G
Petaluma, CA 94954
Library of Congress Catalog Card Number: 80-54225
ISBN-13: 978-0-9605226-0-6
ISBN-10: 0-9605226-0-3
Printed in the United States of America

BUD ALLEN

In memory of a man that we all love
        who's been called home to the heav'ns above

He gave so much to those he held dear
        and in our hearts he'll always be near.

Dad, we love you and that will not change,
        we know you're with God roaming his range

No need for sadness, no need for sorrow
        God holds the key for today and tomorrow

If we talk in God's light, and follow his way
        that's a guarantee, we'll see you someday

WRITTEN BY
JUANITA ALLEN
DAUGHTER—IN—LAW

What would you do if?

ASSUME YOU WORK IN A PRISON.
WHAT WOULD YOU DO IF . . . ?

an inmate of the opposite sex said,
"I think you're beautiful!"

an inmate asks you for a cigarette.

an inmate wants to give you a gift.

a former schoolmate has become a prisoner
assigned to the institution where you are
a custodial officer.

The Dead Sea

The Dead Sea of Israel is a body of water into which rivers flow and become trapped. This unusual landlocked lake *takes* but never *gives*. And because it never gives, its waters cannot sustain any form of life. Still, it has the innocent look of being like any other body of water. Many travelers have been fooled into camping on its shores. They drink of its waters only to wither and die. Yet, in that same area there are lakes that accept and release the river waters. These lakes are teeming with life because they give as well as receive.

Human life can be likened to the Dead Sea and its surrounding bodies of water; people who live rich, fulfilling lives give to their environment and their existence, they do not just take from it. Unless the cycle of give-and-take is completed within a human being, the result will be an arrested individual development. Growth within this person will still occur, but a portion of the mind becomes blocked and does not mature. Takers do know how to give, but their giving is always done with an ulterior motive—they only give for what they can get. People who develop a life style of giving, but who are unable to receive, are very often found in mental institutions: people who take, but cannot or will not give, frequently live outside the law and are often found in prisons.

Men or women in confinement who are trapped at the taking level of life usually continue the style by preying on institution employees. They develop intricate and sophisticated systems of deception, oftentimes for no other reason than the pleasure it provides them. *Takers* must gratify their senses, and the methods they create to receive this gratification are called *set-ups*.

Preface

One might say that the human mind is an organ in need of information to consciously operate, and if deprived of information, it cannot effectively carry out its activities. Laboratory experimenters have long known that by placing people in situations where their eyes and ears have no patterned input, mental activities begin to malfunction. In the same vein, by regulating and filtering a person's information over a period of time, one can alter or distort reasoning—a process also known as manipulation.

The human mind can be manipulated in a variety of ways: fatigue, threat, pain, suffering, isolation, hunger, sleep deprivation and fear are some examples. But the function of the mind may also be influenced by factors not intrinsically harmful. Patterned input to a child such as tales of the baby stork, Santa Claus, and the tooth fairy are examples of fantasy information upon which the mind can operate to create an illusion of grandeur. The boogie man and ghost stories feed information to these young minds that taint their illusion of grandeur with an element of caution. This leaves a feeling of insecurity. Adult patterned information with the intent to manipulate is more complex in that the information fed to a subject must be very believable at this higher level. Feigning sickness to gain someone's sympathy, or spreading untrue or questionable gossip are examples that are sometimes difficult to detect.

The art of manipulating the human thought process to alter behavior is as old as man himself; yet, people are as vulnerable to it today as they were in man's beginning. One of the reasons for this vulnerability is that people set idealistic goals for themselves, and in a reckless desire for goal achievement, they accept information without question when it appears to be consistent with their hopes or beliefs.

For example, from 1970 to 1977, an organization advertising for new inventions claimed they would take a person's idea, manufacture it, and create a market for the new product. People flocked to the organization only to discover there was a high fee involved. Once the fee was paid, the item was never manufactured.

Then there are the bunco artists who dupe men and women out of their life savings. These deceptors convince their victims to withdraw money from their accounts and turn it over to them. The variety of ways for one person to deceive and trick another is limited only by the imagination. Gaining knowledge of psychological manipulation should be the first order of business for every honest citizen, whether involved in criminal justice or not. People in the free society employ the same techniques, varying the application of the steps to fit each particular situation. Case history VI illustrates a recent incident that took place in a small Midwest community, and a more detailed discussion is presented later in this book.

People heading for prison bring their survival trade of manipulation with them and adapt it to the prison environment. Much has been written about manipulation, but this book addresses the specific prison application of this process—a system of deception that is little known by anyone outside of law enforcement, and little understood by employees in the criminal justice system, even though they are the intended victims. Many correctional employees have been told by their supervisors, "They're playing a game on you." The employee fails to see the total picture and cannot orchestrate the seemingly isolated incidents that occur in the game plan. The supervisor sees an isolated situation, but has trouble explaining the total pattern—even though he *knows* it is there. It is a slow, subtle process of manipulation used by prisoners to control the actions of prison employees. In this text, the authors have isolated each step of the system used by convicted felons to coerce prison staff members into breaking the law. They explain how to identify the applied techniques, how to recognize patterned information being fed to them, and once recognized, how to prevent the process from maturing.

Table of Contents

Prologue

The car leaned to the sound of screeching tires as Martha rounded the corner just ten blocks from the hospital where they had taken Joe. Her mind raced from one thought to another: Why would an inmate stab Joe? What could he have done to incite that kind of anger? Joe is a kind, considerate family man. He wouldn't intentionally hurt anyone, so why . . . ? Was there something he hadn't told her? Does Joe display one kind of personality at home and another on the job as she had heard sometimes happens to people in correctional work? There had been a change in Joe over the past few months. He seemed jumpy, restless . . . he had been leaving the house two hours early for work during the past few weeks. Could that have anything to do with the incident?

Her mind pulled her back to the day four years ago when Joe was first informed he was to report to work at a nearby prison. She remembered they joined hands and danced around the room singing and laughing like a couple of young-

1

sters on their first camping trip. Those were happy times. Joe was realizing a life-long dream. He had always wanted to be in law enforcement. "Just think," she recalled him saying, "I'm going to be a correctional officer!" Her thoughts shifted once again to how much Joe's personality had changed recently. They didn't talk to each other the way they used to. He snapped at the children, and now this . . . !

The doctor met Martha in the emergency waiting room. "Joe will be all right," he said, quickly responding to the question being asked by her facial expression. "Only a slight chest wound, no vital organs damaged, he'll be home tomorrow." Martha slumped into a chair sobbing with relief. Joe's captain had been standing nearby, and after Martha regained her composure, he touched her arm and said, "I'm glad he's O.K., Martha." They talked for a moment before seeing Joe.

"I'd ask Joe to get out of corrections if we were not so badly in debt," she told the captain. "But if I know Joe, he'll be back at work before the week is out."

"Well, I'm not sure . . . " Martha noticed an uneasiness as the captain responded to her comment. It bothered her. But she set it aside. Seeing Joe was more important.

Joe had been home over two weeks now and he gave no indication of when he planned to return to work. He seemed distant, deep in thought. Martha didn't want to push after all Joe had just been through—but the debts. . . she would have to say something soon.

It was Sunday; the children had gone out to play. Suddenly Joe said, "Martha, sit down, I need to talk with you." He was obviously worried. She had come to know that expression. It meant bad news. Bracing herself for the worst, Martha sat down.

"Honey, I've been fired! I no longer work for Corrections. I was caught bringing marijuana to a prisoner . . . ." The words didn't come easily, but he went on with the story.

2

"I knew the institution investigator was suspicious of my actions, and that if I didn't stop, he would find out what I was doing, so I told the inmate I would no longer bring things in to him, and he stabbed me."

"But, why?" Martha was confused. Joe had always respected the law. Strong principles, moral values, and honesty were all traits that he exemplified. "I don't understand, Joe," she said. "How could this happen to you?"

Joe continued talking. "About eight months ago, an inmate with whom I had become quite friendly because he liked doing the things I like to do, told me his wife was going to divorce him. I knew something was wrong because his work was falling off, and this fellow was the hardest worker ever assigned to my area. I felt sorry for him. He loved his wife and child, and he didn't want to lose them. He knew I understood the agony he was going through, but it was different for him. He couldn't get out to see his wife. I felt an obligation to help him in some way because he kept me from getting into trouble with my sergeant: I had lost a set of security keys. He found them and returned them to me when I came on duty the next day. He ran quite a risk keeping those keys overnight. Inmates cannot have security keys in their possession, but he didn't want me to get into trouble. I respected him, and because I almost lost you, I understood his problem. Letters from his wife indicated that she still loved him, so he couldn't understand why the talk of divorce. He was emotionally drained. What made the situation worse is that his wife rents an apartment in town not too far from the prison, and he couldn't contact her."

"Doesn't the institution have counselors to help people with their problems?" Martha said.

"I didn't stop to think about that, Martha. I was trying to help the inmate myself. It just seemed like it was my responsibility. I owed him a favor. At any rate, one evening he

3

asked if I would visit his wife on my way home. He felt if his boss told her how hard he was trying to be a good citizen, she would reconsider the divorce. In view of what he'd done for me, I could hardly refuse, now could I?"

Joe continued talking without giving Martha a chance to respond. "I stopped by the apartment that same evening. I told his wife how defenseless her husband felt. She cried, said she still loved him, and the only reason she wanted the divorce was because the baby was ill. She felt that by remarrying she could get proper medical care for the child. I thought how terrible that a young beautiful girl had to suffer in this way. I wrote her a small check, and told her I would drop by frequently to make sure she was O.K. She seemed grateful. I drove by almost nightly for awhile, gave her several more small checks for medication, and she began to feel life was worth living again. It made me feel good to think I was helping a young family in need. One evening she greeted me in her bath robe—said she wasn't feeling well. We talked for awhile; she went to get coffee and suddenly fainted. Her robe had fallen away leaving her partially nude. I wrapped her arms around my neck, placed her on the bed, covered her and called a doctor. He said she was O.K., just exhausted.

"About a week later her husband said, 'You've been visiting my wife a little too frequently; the two of you got something going?' He seemed irritated. I told him I was only trying to help, and he said, 'If you mean that, drop by my house tonight. My wife will give you a package containing marijuana. Bring it to me tomorrow.' No way! I told him. He handed me a letter saying, 'Read that! You got no choice but to do as I tell you!' The letter was addressed to the Superintendent and a copy was to go to you, Martha. It read: 'The officer whose name appears at the top of this document has been visiting my home and paying my wife for sexual favors.' Enclosed were photostatic copies of my personal checks and a photograph of the inmate's wife with her arms around my neck, partially nude and fully awake. I have no idea who took the picture, nor did I realize the fainting spell was a fake. The inmate was right. I had no choice. I did what he told me to do."

To
the
Reader

~~~~~~

Since mankind first conceived the idea of confining the seriously social maladaptive personality in secure detention facilities, conflicts have existed between the people who command and the people who must obey. This causes an indifference toward each other by both parties and has placed a major barrier to the possibility of rehabilitation of inmates. Failure to understand the underlying source of this conflict is failure to recognize prisons for what they represent to the inmates, and what they represent to the people who supervise inmates. It is a story textbooks rarely address, but one that must be told if people interested in the American Criminal Justice System and Corrections are ever to understand why the rehabilitation of law violators is so difficult to achieve. Stepping back in time, we must realize that man has the inherent conflict of identification. Eric Fromm, the noted psychologist, has said, "Man is the only animal who finds his existence a problem which he has to solve and from which he cannot escape." Man becomes anxious over this and needs the answers to six basic but complex human questions.

(1) *Where did I come from?* Each individual is unique and therefore faces the problem of self-awareness. Both male and female Homo sapiens cannot escape meaning when pursuing their values. The way humans answer the question of what life is all about forms the basis of their value system. People are naturally curious about their existence and what brought it about. Those who feel they have found satisfactory answers seem to establish the more appropriate and socially acceptable life styles. They find meaning and purpose in life, develop adequate coping mechanisms, and fulfill their destinations with cooperative attitudes, caring not only for themselves but for others as well. However, there is a group who does not find satisfactory answers to the question of existence; these people become frustrated. They develop inappropriate life styles and seem to exist in a vacuum where rules, morals, and values are sometimes barriers to self-preservation, and they act out against them.

(2) *Why am I here?* People being aware of themselves realize their limitations. They learn to live within these parameters and feel productive and satisfied. Others find their environment can be overwhelming; it gives them a feeling of powerlessness. They become fearful when surrounded by their more capable peers; this makes them anxious over the possible loss of recognition, and they secure their position by circumventing the social system in which they feel caught.

(3) *Who am I?* This can be an extremely revealing question. People who identify with the world around them feel they stand on an important platform. They can identify on the levels of self, intimacy, and group associations. They work and produce. They seem satisfied, have meaningful relationships, interact with others, and enjoy a semblance

7

of happiness. Those who are unable to make this identification develop severe adjustment problems. Their existence has no purpose or meaning and leads them to feel like nonpersons, mere specks in the universe. Self-respect, self-worth, and meaningful relationships elude them and their existence becomes a struggle.

(4) *Where am I going?* Human beings must have goals and direction to fulfill their needs. But more than this, they must have something to strive for which when accomplished will instill a feeling of worth and value—something to be proud of, to admire, and something that provides a sense of completion. People who have no plan or direction, no goals or subgoals develop a "devil may care" attitude and the accomplishments or rights of others become meaningless to them.

(5) *How do I get there?* People must have a means of achieving their goals and subgoals and some sort of action plan that gives meaningful direction. Without a plan, they become fearful of being left behind; survival is threatened, causing them to seek paths that are sometimes harmful to themselves and to others.

(6) *What is my purpose?* The problems of self-awareness, being aware of one's environment, meaning in life, one's position in the spectrum of existence, good and bad, goals and values and direction, can present special concerns in the human process of development when an understanding of these questions seems unachievable. It produces the apathetic person who views life as, "Look out for number one and the heck with everyone else." From this point of reference, criminal practice is an easy transition to make.

THE COPS AND ROBBERS SYNDROME

Once the transition into crime is made and the game of hide and seek is entered into, the conflict and indifference toward accepted society heightens. Policemen develop adverse feelings about people attempting to elude them, and the lawbreakers learn to deeply resent their captors. When criminals are apprehended, they are held in jails pending completion of court procedings. Activity is limited. Because of their short stay, custody and control are emphasized and attempts to rehabilitate practically non-existent. During this holding phase of confinement, the new jail commitment discovers status can be gained among peers if the confinee can devise methods of manipulating or embarrassing an officer and be able to do so without getting into a great deal of trouble. A battle of wits ensues. Policemen and prisoners become even more suspicious and distrustful of each other, which widens the relationship gap between the two factions and the game of hide and seek, cops and robbers continues. If a friendly relationship should occur between an inmate and law enforcement officer during this early confinement stage, it can be quickly dispelled by peers of both groups who accuse the people involved of taking opposite sides.

The Conflict Between the Kept and the Keeper

When the court process has been exhausted and conviction and sentencing to prison pronounced, the confinees enter the prison community preconditioned to animosity, hatred, and disdain for authority. The authors mentioned earlier in this section that people fail to recognize prisons for what they really are. Prisons are totalitarian communities; they are places where people are held against their will and forced to live with their controllers. Freedom of speech, choice, and movement are accomplished under the threat of death—try to escape and tower guards will shoot; they are communitites where one is told when to retire, when to arise, what to wear, what to eat, what attitude to assume, and what is acceptable behavior. Once in prison, members of this society learn that by acting out, refusing to cooperate, devising methods of modifying their keeper's behavior, circumventing or disobeying rules, and being willing to do these things regardless of the punishment, give them status among their peers. Add to this the fact that any inmate who becomes too friendly with a staff member can be labeled a "snitch" or informer and is subject to execution by fellow prisoners. Under this system, there is no reason or incentive which would encourage the type of prisoner/staff relations essential to rehabilitation.

The Conflict Between the Keeper and the Kept

Viewing the dilemma of relationships from the vantage point of staff, prison employees are instructed that their first duty is keeping felons confined for the protection of society, and to do this by whatever means at their disposal. They are immediately trained to enforce rules, administer discipline, and control behavior. Other types of early training are riot control, search techniques, use of force, self-defense, institution security, baton training, tower procedures, escape prevention procedures, and a host of other information that says, "Don't trust prisoners." Like inmates, prison personnel who become too friendly with confinees suffer peer pressure. They are called "ducks" or "convict lovers" and are sometimes suspected of supplying prisoners with illegal contraband simply because of their friendliness. The prisoner contempt for staff causes a reciprocal staff contempt for prisoners; a further separation between staff/inmate relations occurs when prisoners do not appear remorseful over their crimes. Here again, there is no reason or incentive for custody officers to desire friendly relationships with people in confinement.

Bridging the Gap

Yet the custodial department strives to hire correctional personnel who possess a desire to help inmates find a better, more rewarding way of life—people inmates can emulate and learn acceptable habits from—people they can learn to respect and through whom they can find value in their own lives. The convicted residents are displaced from society because of their unacceptable behavior in hopes they will redirect the path they choose to follow. The period in confinement gives them time to think, reevaluate their life goals, and the opportunity to gain life-coping skills and trade skills. This rehabilitation period has changed some inmates' direction toward life and the corrections department is seeking ways to effect more positive changes. The corrections department realizes that people help change people—people who care about people and their welfare help change people for the better. And this is the aim of the confinement period in prison—to help prisoners take stock of their life, goals, and life-style—to help prisoners find acceptable answers to questions that will guide them down a path that is acceptable, satisfying, and rewarding.

Corrections also realizes that people who interact have an influence on each other. Not only does the correctional employee have an influence on the resident, but the opposite may happen. To guard against any negative outcomes of these interactions, the department has laid some ground rules for these interactions to assure positive outcomes. Employees must also live by additional rules in this confined society. These rules were not capriciously contrived but were wisely created to direct interactions with wisdom.

Some of these rules direct employees to be friendly, but not overly familiar; to help the inmates with communication, but not to personally take out letters, even though there appears to be nothing the matter with them; to give or accept nothing to or from inmates unless authorized by the supervisor or job assignment; to give advice when needed or requested, but not to share personal data or information with inmates. These are just some of the rules and to the uninitiated, these rules may seem trivial and unnecessary, but the rules were made to counteract the pitfalls some employees may encounter.

The inmates know they are not going to listen to someone unless there exists mutual respect, example, admiration, cooperation, proper attitude, enthusiasm, and idealism. The inmates know the rules, in some cases, better than the employees. When an inmate breaks a rule, he expects the employee to follow the law enforcement continuum of

Crime → Detection → Apprehension → Conviction → Punishment

The employee must follow this process to show the resident he will not be allowed to get away with unacceptable behavior. Prisoners have no respect for staff members they can lower to their own level of behavior. They do maintain great respect for people who, regardless of pressure, can continue to provide a high level of dignity and professionalism—people they can emulate. Employees follow the standard law enforcement continuum when necessary but adopt a new continuum in the prison setting that tends to heighten good behavior and treatment. Inmates want control—self-control that will become so innate they can carry it back to the free society with them. For them, a good habit must be tried, then supported by staff, not allowing nonsense to intercede. An employee will follow a new behavior scheme of

Observation → Recognition → Prevention → Treatment

This approach addresses behavior before—not after the fact, thereby making control and treatment easier for everyone with no one being caught or embarrassed because no violation was committed. By dispelling the nonsense of deception, the prisoner is released from temptation, and both keeper

12

and kept can be about the business of treatment.

When an employee circumvents the rules, the prisoners lose respect for this person's ability to help them. The game of cops and robbers re-ignites, and the inmate and staff member lose any possibility of real rehabilitation interactions. When the keeper fails to follow rules, the kept are calling the shots—not the employee, even though this keeper may think he or she is bending the rules to help an inmate in a special situation. The inmates figure that if an employee will give an inch in violating minor rules, why not throw rehabilitation to the wind and try to take the mile. This book explains the subtle ways the inmates test to see if they can extend the inch and gain peer status and contraband. It also explains how employees can regain control and respect even if they have extended themselves an inch or two or three. Once control and respect is regained, the path to rehabilitation is again possible. It also explains what happens if an employee allows the inch to extend into a mile. The employee is in trouble, and the involved inmates are in trouble. Everyone loses. Yet it is a game that all inmates recognize, and one that some cannot resist if presented the opportunity to play. This book intends to show the extent to which manipulators will proceed if unchecked. Inmates are susceptible to the lure in manipulation for self-satisfaction, and people unschooled in this process remain vulnerable to inmates' subtle, coercive tactics. It is hoped that by displaying the full scope of the process, that prison employees and anyone else encountering it will recognize it in its infancy and put a stop to the nonsense. This critical examination of these controlling techniques cut through vain speculation. It reveals the subtlety of deception by providing a tool for recognizing and reckoning with these manipulative processes.

Also presented are models based on actual case histories in which highly resistant captives confront their victims and

13

through a careful process of subtle inducements manage to compromise them. The purpose here is to provide the realism necessary for critical examination so prison administrators and employees can effectively control illicit behavior before it proceeds to the point illustrated in the models. The case in the prologue is an example of how one person can artfully manage or control another person through the shrewd use of unfair fraudulent influence. In this case, over two years passed before anyone knew for sure who was managing whom. Was Joe telling Martha the truth? Both the inmate and his wife testified that Joe manipulated them, that he took advantage of the woman's poverty circumstances by offering money for sex and pacified the husband with supplies of marijuana. It was finally cleared up when the inmate became involved with a prisoner church affiliated prayer group. Part of his new orientation required the confession of past crimes. Among other confessions, he admitted that Joe had told the truth.

It is the authors' contention that if inmates can identify employees who are susceptible to manipulation, then staff can do likewise; that once identified, steps can be taken to educate prison employees on the techniques of deception and prevention necessary to extend them another effective and productive control tool. The authors talked personally with employees who stated they were on their way out of their correctional careers but decided to remain in the profession after receiving training in techniques of recognizing and preventing manipulation of their behavior. They indicated the information permitted them to retake control of their area, gain prisoner respect, and markedly improve their performance reports. People with this training can easily deal with the situation without alienating their provocateurs and quickly progress with the treatment process.

The authors further realize that by providing staff

14

members with a knowledge of deception and fraudulent manipulation, they are aiding in the goal of prisoner rehabilitation. Prisoners who manipulate for self-satisfaction or personal gain do not find the end result inwardly rewarding even though they openly verbalize the opposite of being true. Inwardly they have a deep suppressed desire to be socially accepted and to develop acceptable patterns of behavior, but this is often overshadowed by early hedonistic and sensualistic cravings which develop into a belief that satisfying the senses is of primary importance. Many people who commit crimes are deeply remorseful once the crime is committed; yet they add to the remorse with the commission of additional crimes. With respect to this behavior, a few prisoners verbalize what most of them feel by saying, "Help me control myself!" This is said in many ways.

On one occasion, an officer became disgusted with an inmate who refused to behave and said, "Your dad should have beat the daylights out of you!" to which the inmate replied, "My dad didn't like me that much!" A great deal can be read into the inmate's reply, but mostly he is saying, "I am not satisfied with my behavior and if you like me you will help me control myself." This, then, is the main purpose of *Games Criminals Play*. By detailing and exposing this manipulative process, the authors will have helped inmates in their desire for aid in self-control.

Never to our knowledge has there been an attempt to systematize illicit behavior control of prison staff members by inmates and never before in corrections has anyone isolated and explained the subtle, step-by-step process. The authors advocate using the prevention continuum whenever possible as this develops good staff/inmate relationships. To aid the student of correctional science in the area of recognition in the continuum, the next section contains pointers of staff and inmate terms along with expected custodial competence.

An employee's actions and those actions alone will determine the opinions that are formed of the staff member by the inmates. Whether staff likes it or not, the critical eye of the inmate is a twenty-four hour companion. However, if staff realizes from the beginning that success in any field is only achieved through accomplishment, progress, and dignity, then they can calculate their efforts to make this possible. The onlooker will see an employee who is friendly, self-assured, self-reliant, and who exudes a commanding confidence without the slightest hint of brusqueness or conceit. The ward will observe staff members to see how they can be of help—either in a gullible, defeating way, or in a positive, constructive manner for which they were hired. The constructive employee will combine friendliness, courtesy, firmness, sympathy, and calm efficiency, will learn to react in a friendly, tactful manner, and will meet any emergency with cool-headed composure.

The correctional employee is given the responsibility of rebuilding, retraining, and restoring. It takes enthusiasm, dedication, and a desire to work. This employee is charged with the task of correcting, rectifying, altering, and adjusting; but more than this, he or she assists the ward in bringing problems to the surface and then aids in the development of habits that are designed to be socially beneficial and that will restore self-respect. The constructive keeper learns to serve the charges as advisor, friend, confidant, counselor, moderator, and when necessary, disciplinarian. When something must be denied, it is firmly but politely refused. This staff member develops a keen sense of awareness and judgment that stems from the "firm but fair" philosophy of reasoning. This correctional person will not be easily provoked or manipulated into situations that distract because to do so might jeopardize personal safety or the safety of others, and it would lessen the example to be set.

Definitions
and
Terms

~~~~~~

DEFINITIONS FOR STAFF

Almost everyone knows the dictionary definition of words like naive, friendliness and professionalism, but few people realize the importance of these terms as they relate to corrections, or the ramifications not understanding them can have on correctional employees. In detention facilities these terms are bandied about freely without adequate explanation. The admonishment of "Don't be naive", comes immediately for the new staff member, which seems to mean if a decision made by that employee fails to accomplish its purpose the individual is naive. Warnings against excessive friendliness and over-familiarity are frequent admonishments, but there are no guidelines to follow. Actions that one supervisor may view as overly friendly another may not. Finally, prison personnel are told to "Be professional," but what is professionalism?

17

Before further discussion can be meaningful, it is necessary to arrive at some sort of workable definition of these terms as they relate to the people who must apply them.

Naiveté

Staff members who become overly-familiar with inmates are said to be naive. The actual meaning of the word is "having or displaying a simple or trusting nature; lacking in experience, lacking in careful judgment or analysis, and being unsophisticated." Most people entering corrections have a simple or trusting nature. They hear and believe inmate stories, then act upon their information. If they become disillusioned, bitterness sets in and their effectiveness as correctional employees declines. The suffering stems from lack of experience. Experience takes time, but a simple and trusting nature can become sophisticated at once. The solution is simple—before acting on information supplied by men in confinement, employees should check it out. By reading inmate files and asking staff members who know these offenders if the information is reliable, they will not allow the dishonest ones to destroy their judgment by fixing their mind on one avenue of thought. They will be aware that not all inmates are honest and not all inmates are dishonest.

Careful judgment refers to the ability of employees to analyze not only the movements, words, and actions of inmates, but their own as well. Recently, in one institution, an inmate said to a female employee, seemingly in jest, "If I had one wish, I'd wish to go home with you." The remark seemed innocent enough, but her response to the statement was to come back to haunt her. She replied, "I doubt if the institution would approve of that," and they shared a good laugh. The indication to the inmate was that if it were not for the dictates of the institution, she would approve. He spent long hours building in his mind what he thought was a relationship that had exceeded the bounds of friendship and one day he attempted to compromise her. During the investigation that followed, the employee stated, "A more careful choice of words would have prevented all this."

As the readers continue through this book, it may be interesting for them to envision how they would act and react in similar circumstances.

Friendliness and Over-familiarization

Excessive friendliness and over-familiarization are also common terms in corrections. Professional people usually display a friendly personality and corrections expects their employees to be that way. However, inmates often see this trait as a weakness unless the employee can make a distinction between friendliness and familiarity. In the Spanish language there are familiar and unfamiliar friendships, distinguished by the familiar and unfamiliar "you: tu and usted." People administer them with the same courtesy, the same pleasant attitude and the same politeness. But before people can be familiar friends, they must be loyal, honest, and proven, which involves time, effort, and the right circumstances, situation or group. All other friendships are unfamiliar.

Correctional employees are overly-familiar if they allow the taking of license or liberties. Such things as discussing their personal problems or financial matters would come in this category. Discussions of sexual problems would be the same. If they permit inmates to address them by their first names or they address inmates by theirs, they open the door to familiar friendship. This seemingly insignificant act permits inmates to take greater license than they would take with staff members who do not permit the privilege.

In one institution, a former street gang leader who had become a minister confirmed that the initial breakdown of professionalism is for an employee to go on a first name basis with an inmate. "All gang leaders," he said, "are aware of this." The California prison system, as indicated in their Directors Rules, permits this type of familiarization if the inmate and employee agree. However, the reader should be aware that in the majority of cases studied, employees who were dismissed for wrong doings permitted the use of first names at the early stages of the manipulative process. Correctional employees should maintain an attitude of helpfulness much the same as shared between doctors and their patients. Doctors may be viewed as the finest of people, but they do not share their personal problems, their finances, their aches and pains or their personal life with people they serve. They maintain a professional barrier. They are unfamiliar friends.

Enforcing rules for some inmates but relaxing them for others is not only inconsistent and unfair, it is another form of over-familiarity. Promising favors that are not within a staff member's jurisdiction to grant is the same as accepting favors that lead to the taking of liberties, which can lead to the employee becoming the object of a set-up. Later, if this person becomes the object of peer criticism, this employee is said to be naive.

In one institution, a Medical Technical Assistant (MTA) had become overly friendly with his inmate orderly and frequently shared extra food from his lunch box with the man. One evening he gave the orderly a piece of rolled salami about two inches long. A few evenings later, the inmate suggested that the MTA bring a still larger piece because it was not sold in the inmate canteen, and he would like to share some with his buddies. The following night the employee brought him a full roll. Not long after that, the inmate told the MTA to bring in drugs, saying he had the salami as evidence of rules violation, and he would report the incident if the medic failed to comply. In this case, the employee did not comply. Instead, he reported the inmate to the captain, saying, "I made a stupid mistake and this inmate is trying to capitalize on it." The captain complimented the MTA for sharing the incident in the face of what he thought would be criticism, and told him the lesson would make him a better employee.

Criteria of a Profession

Many correctional employees have the impression that the task they perform is somewhere in between skilled and unskilled labor. So, before discussing professionalism as such, its precise classification needs to be determined. It is by understanding one's station in life that professional personalities develop. First of all, correctional skills emanate from a learned effort, and the distinctive mark of a profession, as opposed to unskilled labor, is its emphasis on learning. Secondly, extensive study, frequent change, and a constant accumulation of understanding identify a profession. The earliest of the professions consisted of theology, medicine, and all branches of law enforcement. The qualifications of a profession may be outlined as follows:

A. Every true profession has a specialized terminology, a professional "universe of discourse."

B. Every profession requires a special body of knowledge and skill as a basis for uniform performance of its standard practices and procedures. These practices are voluntarily understood and accepted by members of the profession as appropriate under given circumstances.

C. The practices are based on specialized training and on conscious research and study.

D. The sharing and acquiring of information is one of the most important aspects of a profession, and like all professions, it maintains a continuous flow of professional literature.

E. All professions require a high degree of personal responsibility on the part of each individual member, which is coupled with a similar freedom and independence of action.

F. All professions require a high degree of allegiance to its many facets, its code of ethics, and to the public interest.

Corrections, then, most assuredly meets and even exceeds the criteria of a profession. But, simply identifying corrections as a profession is not enough. Each individual member of the organization must also practice the concept of professionalism.

Professionalism

Professionalism in corrections is a word used to admonish a specific attitude and job approach. In its strictest sense, it refers to communicating and acting in a manner that distinguishes a person of skill and knowledge from an amateur. Professionalism is a state of mind: a type and style of dignity.

If correctional employees ever aspire to achieve a high degree of professionalism, they must first believe themselves capable of the accomplishment. They are what they think they are—nothing more, nothing less. If they believe a certain task is impossible, then for them, it will be impossible. On the other hand, if they believe no accomplishment is too great, their achievements will amaze everyone. The feeling of self-worth develops the natural traits of self-confidence and self-assuredness, and as these traits are being perfected, mental and emotional stability reward the practitioner. An attitude follows that governs speech, actions and movements, which, in turn, develops a type and style of dignity to fit the individual personality.

Everyone knows people who possess traits they admire—

one has toughness and "grit", another has reliability and steadfastness, and perhaps another has dedication to a cause. But every now and then there comes a person who seems to have "put it all together." This person is a model, a true example, a professional.

Few, if any, of the people hiring into corrections enter as professionals. The various departments ask not that they possess the traits listed below when they become correctional employees but that they be willing to set them as their goals. Professionals are capable of:

... believing in themselves and exuding self confidence without the slightest hint of brusqueness or conceit.

... being reliable and emotionally stable; able to accept responsibility and take independent action.

... controlling their situation instead of their situation controlling them.

... being firm but fair which means adherence to the rules in a patient, constructive, creative manner.

... being not anxious to impress or cherish inflated ideas of their own importance.

... displaying good manners and speech.

... being unselfish and not touchy.

... searching for truth instead of spreading rumors or gossip.

... not keeping account of evil or gloating over the wickness of others.

... being neat in appearance and developing a friendly personality without becoming overly-familiar.

... analyzing their own speech and actions as well as the speech and actions of others.

... being humble, sympathetic and understanding without divulging their own personal affairs or problems, or without allowing themselves to be distracted or given to favoritism.

... adapting to change, maintaining enthusiasm, dispelling prejudice, and showing allegiance to their employers.

... being alert, quick to respond, able to make decisions accurately and fairly, and concerned with the welfare of both staff and inmates.

The acquisition of these fourteen steps to professionalism does not come easily. It requires hard work, dedication, and training. The employee who just puts in time to collect a wage, abuses sick leave, or becomes bitter, ignores the path to professionalism achievement and this action will not only jeopardize personal safety, but the safety of others as well.

It is rare to find an employee who has perfected the art of being professional because it is a constantly changing art requiring daily self-evaluation and reorientation of goals and purpose. On the other hand, it is common to find employees in the process of developing these professional stages. There is a saying that states: "You become like the company you keep." If it is difficult for an employee of corrections to find staff members engaged in the practice of professionalism, it is because those employees are not themselves engaged in the practice. However, the moment they begin developing its features, they will suddenly notice practicing professionals all around them. As mentioned before, new employees in corrections are naturally naive in some areas because they lack experience, but this does not mean that they must be overly-familiar or unprofessional in their dealings with inmates. Simply by applying the concept of the unfamiliar friendship, the correctional novice will better understand how professionalism can be achieved.

Custodial Competence and Expectations
as Related to Professionalism

Professionalism and competence are contiguous with law enforcement goals and expectations. By developing good habit patterns, one becomes a professional. These traits cannot be acquired simply by time and experience, but must be desired and actively pursued. The accomplishment of professionalism and competence in law enforcement differs from most other organizations because employee demands and expectations are unique. In most large organizations or professions, competence is acquired by a constant process of doing, and professionalism is achieved by predetermined modes of behavior. But in law enforcement, a new set of standards can be required for each situation that arises, for each new job assignment, or for each promotional level. A street policeman may develop friendships with people on his beat that an undercover detective would be unable to emulate. A policeman or correctional S.W.A.T. Team member would have a different attitude and job approach than a juvenile officer. A prison custodial officer promoting to correctional counselor would become decidedly more familiar with inmates than is usually permitted in security phases of correctional employment. And, all of these people would be required to maintain different sets of professional standards when apprehending a criminal, quelling riots, or preventing escapes. A doctor or lawyer can follow a predefined set of rules to accomplish professional goals, but in law enforcement those rules must very often be made up by the individual officer at the time an incident occurs. Because each emergency may present a different crisis, there is no way to predetermine how one should or will act in a given situation, especially when that situation involves a life threat. Suggestions can be made, but no one knows how he or she will react until facing that emergency. Onlookers may easily criticize the professionalism or competence of a policeman or correctional officer because they rarely, if ever, face life and death situations.

Another demand placed upon law enforcement personnel requires quick emotional changes. A person who has just used physical force to prevent someone from being injured or killed must quickly make the transition from action to understanding when dealing with innocent bystanders. The switch from sternness to pacification involves sets of professional standards that are extremely difficult to achieve. After years of working under this kind of tension, people in law enforcement tend to seek positions on the force with limited emergencies. Once out of these areas of stress, they may relax to a point of complacency and become vulnerable to manipulation. They are "burned out," tired of the hassle, and relax their guard. People in custodial functions who become complacent can easily cause routine duties to become so routine that they set aside caution. This is especially true of correctional employees. In prisons, complacency usually develops at a much earlier stage than in other branches of law enforcement because of the monotonous routine most of the institutional work entails. There is a constant procession of counts, feeding of inmates, supervision of housing areas and job assignments, and a host of other functions where daily routine never varies.

To anyone interested in corrections as a career, or to people actively engaged in the profession, the importance of guarding against complacency must be stressed because lax employees fail to notice signs that spell potential trouble. Contrary to what has been expressed in some correctional institutions or county jails by administrators, fights, riots and killings do not simply happen. These things have roots that are usually long nurtured. Unless effective, alert officers notice the warning signals, major disturbances will occur. Some of the warning signs that point to situations which can quickly degenerate into uncontrolled circumstances are listed below.

Warning Signals
Tension increase
* A noticeable general uneasiness of prison population.
* An unusual silence in the movies, mess hall, gym or wherever large numbers of prisoners are permitted to congregate.

* An increase in both the number and sensational nature of rumors from inmates.

Attitude change
* A poor attitude among inmates who are normally congenial.
* Protesting and name calling.
* A large scale refusal of inmates to obey orders.
* An increase in incidents of property destruction.
* An increasing number of incidents or threats of violence among inmates.
* The increase of occurrences of threatening or insulting remarks made to staff by inmates on a large scale.

Grouping
* Unauthorized groupings.
* Spectators gathering in yard perimeters when small inmate groupings are occurring.
* The voluntary disbursal of small inmate groups when they see an officer approaching.

Activity decrease
* A sudden lack of participation in sports activities.
* An increase in the number of people reporting to sick call.
* A large scale refusal to cooperate in institution programs.
* Leaders enticing others not to work.
* Large scale refusal to work.

Battle Ready
* Segregation of races
* Excessive purchases at the canteen. Prisoners know in advance of trouble that they will be confined to their rooms until peace is restored so they stock up on food.
* The sudden lack of radios, tape recorders, musical instruments in areas where inmates normally have these things— they do not want them destroyed when the incident occurs.
* A decrease in the number of reported incidents of

drug usage. In all jails or prisons, inmates find ways of smuggling drugs into the institutions. A sudden decrease in the usage occurs because a person needs to be alert to protect his own life if an incident occurs.

* An unusual number of inmates remaining awake at night (lookout).
* Inmates sleeping in their clothing (battle ready).
* Inmates who wear two or three sets of clothing during cold or warm weather. (Battle jackets to prevent injury.)

As word of impending violence and excitement spreads through rumor, gang leaders detach momentarily to recruit. Bystanders are forced into the incident through peer pressure. As groups enlarge, gang leaders encourage dangerous behavior. They send messages from one group to another, and people begin to move around aimlessly. An undercurrent of excitement, uncertainty and testing develops as group members contact each other. Confusion and tension become more obvious. In terms of inmate groupings, when the frenzy of tension reaches a feverish pitch, a precipitating event will occur. The precipitating event may not be serious by itself (protesting or name calling) but if it takes place at a time when tension is at its peak, the stage for a riot has been set. Some time has been spent detailing these warning signs because it has long been known that the complacent officer, the nonprofessional, becomes so steeped in routine that the obvious goes unnoticed and prison incidents occur.

Another part of professionalism is integrity. Without integrity, no one can experience the feeling of accomplishment, pride in one's daily performance, or the sense of knowing a job has been well done. In corrections, integrity means the employee always keeps his or her word to an inmate or peers. Promises that cannot be kept should never be made. The loss of integrity leads to complacency and some typical traits shown below develop when integrity is lost.

A. Leaving part of one's work for the other person.
B. Discussing inappropriate subjects with or in front of inmates.
C. Passing the buck.
D. Chronic complaining.
E. Loss of pride in appearance.
F. Making excuses.
G. Abuse of sick leave.
H. Inappropriate or unprofessional conduct.
I. Excessive drinking during off-duty hours.
J. Sloppy security habits.

As mentioned before, professionalism is a daily, on-going feature of law enforcement that one never takes for granted. It is maximum performance, making an effort to know and understand procedures, always being prepared and alert, and never assuming you know it all. It is the "know-it-all" or complacent employee that becomes a prime target for manipulation.

By understanding the terms discussed in this section, DEFINITIONS FOR STAFF, the reader can more clearly see how practicing professionals are less likely to be victimized than their more gullible or lax counterparts. To this point, terms that relate to employees have been explored. There are also some inmate terms that need to be understood.

INMATE TERMS

Modifying behavior for criminal intent requires aid. Team effort makes detection of a set-up more difficult because one participant can verify the acts of another, and suspicion can be momentarily set aside. On the other hand, individual deception is largely devoid of participant verification, so tracing a suspicion can be more easily accomplished by staff. The size of a set-up team will depend on the goal to be accomplished, the personality characteristics of the victim, the possible time involved, and the location and physical layout of the area where the manipulation will take place.

A well structured set-up team encompasses observers, contacts, runners, turners, and pointmen, each with a specific task to perform.

Observers

Inmate observers in a set-up process watch and listen to a potential victim. They theorize by a person's actions and the things that a person says whether or not he or she would be a good candidate for selection. Observers pay particular attention to employees who use inmate jargon, ignore minor rule infractions, play favorites—enforce rules for some and not for others—or are easily distracted.

Contacts

Inmate contacts supply information about an employee. A former clerk or orderly who knows the staff member's work-style would be an excellent contact. Inmates who overhear personal conversations between the employee and other staff members, and who have formed opinions about certain strengths and weaknesses possess valuable data. These people also ask subtle questions of any talkative staff members and gain additional information about their intended victim. Interestingly, prisoners who do not condone the manipulation process wrought upon staff are pressured into cooperating with team members as far as supplying information such as employee work habits, likes and dislikes, etc. These prisoners are actually relieved when the prospective victim renders the information useless by allowing no nonsense and displaying professional qualities. An employee who prevents a set-up gains further respect from the inmates by not allowing the pressured prisoner information to be used in a harmful or derogatory manner. Inmates find out mountains of information about employees. To be able to effectively use it against them rests in the employee's hands—not the inmates'.

Runners

Inmate runners are not active members of the total set-up process, but will assist in any phase of it for some sort of reward. Payment is usually drugs, money, cigarettes, and the promise of sex when a woman has been the victim of a compromise scheme. Runners are usually the only ones paid because they must expose themselves to the employee by asking for small items like cigarettes, pencils or by acting out some minor rule violation.

The observers and contacts do not risk this exposure and may not even be known by the victim. The inmate grapevine exemplifies an effective communication system and the sharing of this kind of information is expected as well as given status.

Turners

Turners befriend employees and use that friendship to ultimately coerce them into engaging in infractions of the rules. The team chooses an inmate from their group that seems to fit the victim's likes or personality and bestows on him the title of "turner." This inmate will be the least suspected by the person to be victimized because the turner works very hard at establishing a close bond, using whatever methods to which the intended victim is susceptible. The turner tries to portray only good qualities to the victim and uses runners to ascertain that person's reaction to undesirable qualities. The turner tries to get a lever or hold on the intended victim either by use of a runner or by his own subtle techniques. A lever is an important step in the set-up and may be acquired at any point along with way. The process of turning begins when a staff member looks the other way and allows the taking of license or liberties.

Pointmen

Inmate pointmen stand guard when an employee is in the process of granting illegal favors, violating institution rules, or is being compromised or harmed. For example, an officer in one institution was coerced into bringing alcohol for inmates. While they were drinking, a pointman stood outside the area ready to drop a book to warn of other approaching staff. In another case, the pointman left his post to partake of the contraband. Custody discovered the illegal scenario and immediately took appropriate action.

Trouble Spot

Trouble spots are areas of job assignments where staff members have or can be turned into "mules" or "packhorses." Prisoners know it is only a matter of time before both they and their supplier are caught, so when receiving work assignments to the trouble spot, they must decide whether or not to become involved. It is a pressure decision: "Do I want to share in the spoils and face punishment, or should I just do my own time and find a different assignment?" Most inmates realize the temptation would be too much for them to handle.

The
Set-Up

~~~~~~

This section deals with the actual set-up process. It should be noted that a set-up is understood either partially or in its entirety by all prison inmates. However, we must emphasize once again that even though inmates recognize manipulation, not all inmates engage in the practice. But research has shown that a significant number of them do. The practice is becoming a serious problem for prison employees and an extremely popular pastime for inmates because of the gained peer status when their victim performs illegal acts for them. The inmates boast they turned their subject. Also, the physical rewards such as sharing illegal contraband or sex in the case of a female victim motivate inmates into engaging in this type of behavior.

The following steps of behavioral manipulation are designed to show the reader how inmates implement this outlined set-up. It should be understood that this process does not always develop in the order shown, but all the elements will usually be utilized regardless of the procedure inmates employ. The steps appear in an intricately interwoven manner, thus making initial separation of the steps difficult. Victims have trouble seeing the pattern because they only recognize a strand—not the whole design. But once each piece receives a label and its relationship to other pieces are laid out, recognition of the total picture or any part of it should be simple.

Even seasoned employees who have learned to play or cope with the game can benefit from this book. It may explain how they act instinctively in the prison setting. And it may also help them better relay the message, "They are playing a game on you," in detail to someone who needs it.

The fourteen set-up steps incorporate three processes: the beginning two processes weave the net to catch the victim for the final process—the inmate payoff. The first three steps explain the *techniques,* a process which depicts the inmates' modus operandi used in the set-up. The next eight steps contain the *tools,* a process which describes the inmates' resources used to turn the employee. The final three steps culminate in the *turnout,* a process used to actually compromise employees and leave them in real trouble.

An outline of the process is presented to give an overview of the procedure, and to be used later as a quick review or reference if the need ever arises.

An employee who understands the process possesses the necessary skills to stop the set-up at once. Some previous, untrained employees have not been so fortunate.

TECHNIQUES OF A SET-UP

I. The Observation Step
   A. Body language observation
      1. body movements
      2. nervousness/ease
      3. manner of dress
   B. Listening observation
      1. places of gathered information
         a. snack bar conversation
         b. phone conversation
         c. hallway or tier conversation
      2. kinds of gathered information
         a. likes/dislikes
         b. personal data
         c. personal history
   C. Verbal observation
      1. inmate conversation with proposed victim
         a. confirm listening observation
         b. gather more information
      2. inmate suggestion of minor rule infraction
         a. approval/disapproval
         b. employee control/uncomfortable signs
   D. Action observation
      1. inmate actually violates a minor rule
      2. tests include employee's
         a. method of command
         b. response to emergencies
         c. view of job
II. Selection of a Victim
   A. Intentional selection
      1. excessive friendliness and over-familiarity
      2. naive and trusting nature

3. gullibility or weakness
4. suggestibility or lack of experience
B. Accidental selection
1. hidden weakness
2. change of job assignment or family status
C. Pegging employees
1. soft
2. hard
3. mellow
III. Test of Limits and/or Fish Testing
A. Test of Limits
1. quarter-step pace
2. constant nudge of rules
a. test opinions and theories
b. test tolerance levels
c. test personality characteristics
i.e. can you refuse?
3. testing becomes serious
B. Fish testing
1. asking for things not supposed to be given
2. persistence

Tools of a Set-Up

IV. The Support System
A. Ego uplifting
1. offer of help
2. setting loyalty standards
3. you're the best
4. pledge of faith and devotion
5. strengthening the friendship
B. Reliance on inmate to make job easier
1. developing trust
2. the indispensable inmate

        3. loss of effective control

V. Empathy and/or Sympathy

   A. Empathy

        1. projecting one's personality onto another

        2. sharing similar problems

        3. understanding

        4. the you/me syndrome

        5. pegging emotions, responses, etc.

        6. seeking levels of identification

   B. Sympathy

        1. sameness of feelings

        2. victim's response to pity

        3. level of compassion

VI. Plea for Help

   A. Rehabilitation—change of life style

        1. I need you

        2. I'm a failure/I lack confidence

        3. you are the only one who can help

           a. tragic event

           b. "one-time-only" rule violation

   B. Confidentiality

        1. share with someone

        2. keep it out in the open

VII. The We/They Syndrome

   A. Separate victim from staff

        1. they don't understand you, but we do

        2. they're wrong about you

        3. they're treating you like they treat us

        4. pitting one staff member against another

        5. I'm O.K., you're O.K.—they're not O.K.

   B. Similar background

        1. ethnic

        2. neighborhood

        3. circumstance

VIII. Offer of Protection
    A. Minor offers
        1. friendliness and trust
        2. I'll take the heat
        3. I won't let that happen to you
    B. Serious offers
        1. use of fear
        2. staging an event
        3. a grateful victim
IX. Allusion to Sex
    A. If the victim is female
        1. the intent/the urge
        2. allusions "out there"/nice guy image
        3. employee response
            a. no comment
            b. confinees are like that
            c. tell me more
            d. I've had enough
        4. institution procedures
        5. effect of rumors
    B. If the victim is male
        1. coercion
        2. used as lever
        3. job security
X. The Touch System
    A. If the victim is female: caution
        1. flicking or bumping
        2. pat on the back
        3. prolongation
        4. the accident
    B. If the victim is male: form bond
        1. friendly nudge
        2. slap on the back

XI. The Rumor Clinic
    A. Pulling staff away from the victim
        1. planting the seed
        2. the street psychologist
        3. peer attitudes
    B. The result
        1. employee isolation
        2. rejection
        3. inmates—the only friends

Turnouts

XII. The Shopping List
    A. Contraband or favor demand
        1. coercion
        2. sales pitch/"one-time-only"
        3. drugs, alcohol, money, sex
    B. Employee reaction
        1. disbelief
        2. time for decision
    C. Inmate exposure
        1. risk disciplinary action
        2. no turning back
XIII. The Lever
    A. Creation of the lever
        1. obtained anytime during set-up
        2. "aware"/unaware
        3. generated out of "friendship"
    B. Usages
        1. psychological threat
        2. inmates risk further disciplinary action
    C. Employee reaction
        1. acceptance/refusal
        2. personality changes

3. it is only a matter of time

XIV. The Sting

    A. Force

        1. physical threat

        2. battle of the minds

        3. physical harm

    B. Power position

        1. inmate control of others

        2. loss of autonomy feared by inmates

TECHNIQUES OF A SET-UP

THE OBSERVATION PROCESS

Observation, naturally, begins the process in the set-up procedure. Manipulation cannot take place without a victim, and victims are not just capriciously selected. The results of a careful, close, silent study by the inmates determine the likelihood of a victim selection. Good shoppers look around and compare: they want the best return for their vested interest. Employees become vulnerable and unsuspecting to the multitude of subtle techniques convicts develop to read them. Their movements, words, and actions supply these manipulators with a great deal of information vital to the set-up process. From employee responses to seemingly harmless questions, inmates formulate staff personality profiles and decide which prison staff members might bend or circumvent institution rules and regulations. Manipulators soon learn which employees distract easily and allow illegal activities to go unnoticed. They know where to place individual tolerance levels and which staff members can probably be coerced into granting favors or bringing illegal contraband into their institutions.

Formal education has nothing to do with their knowledge of games. For example, an inmate, reading on a second grade level, orally read a story about a bunco artist. After four pages he was asked by the teacher, "What's happening in the story?" to which he replied, "He's being real nice to the lady." The teacher said, "Come on, what's really happening?!" An excited smile broke out on the respondant's face, "He's playing a game on her!" Even though many inmates do not buy into the game, there remains no doubt they all understand the process.

Inmates make determinations about prison employees because their movements, language, and actions compare to a color spectrum. Colors have shades of light and dark with intervening hues. So, too, does the way people move, speak, and act. Because of these variations or shades of meaning, psychologists, for example, can map personalities and be amazingly accurate in their predictions. On the basis of how people walk, talk and act, they find it even possible to delve into people's innermost thoughts and feelings. Because personality traits lend themselves to interpretation, one need not be a person of letters to seek and discover hidden messages. Inmates become very proficient in this ability. They incorporate it into their trade. Within a very short time after confinement, they learn to read staff members with almost the same accuracy as the psychologist. They read the signs prison employees post, and from these messages decide who among them will be receptive to a set-up.

Formalization of the study seems nonexistent in that there is no written work. Information gathered and stored in the minds of team members originates by the observation of *body language* and the *listening observation.* From this information, opinions are formed, theories created, and characteristics categorized. Then the team develops modification procedures which reflect the victim's responses to the continuous verbal and action observations.

Body Language

The manner and method in which correctional employees carry themselves give off messages. The astute onlooker wants to know if the employee is unsure in a situation, if there is a lack of confidence, if there exists a dislike for the job, if a situation can instill fear, and a myriad of other personality traits. Actions such as the tugging at the ear lobe, biting the lip or fingernails, the constant folding and unfolding of the arms at inappropriate times, not knowing what to do with the hands, excessive scratching, shifting from foot to foot when one should be standing still, or a washing of the hands motion all display nervous actions that under certain conditions can convey a variety of messages. Conversely, the steepling of one's fingers, leaning back in a chair and crossing one's legs, or leaning forward by bracing the face with one's hands and resting the elbows on a desk or table can exemplify the impression of ease. Walking is an inherited trait, but even this has enough variation to indicate the demeanor felt on a certain day or situation.

One's attire can also transmit body language messages. Unpressed clothing, a partial uniform, or buttons left open indicate sloppiness and could be interpreted as inattention to detail. Inmates may assume from this that a person will allow the taking of liberties. Low cut blouses, mini skirts, and hyphenated walking motions send a message of availability whether intended or not. Manipulators read these messages and make determinations about them. Employees should be aware of their own body language.

Listening Observation

"All my husband wants to do is sleep." This statement jokingly and innocently came out during a snack bar conversation with a friend. An inmate, in the process of delivering breakfast to the two women, construed the comment as a message to him of the woman's unhappiness at home, and he subsequently began hiding love notes under her plate. Some inmates demonstrate this egocentricity, and a particular inmate may believe that conversations contain hidden messages for him alone.

Whether prison staff members like it or not, their conversations are constantly monitored. By not being aware of who is listening or how their words can be interpreted, staff may very well provide the foundation for selection as a set-up victim. Team members need input for their early evaluation of the personality profile. They want to find predictable patterns they can rely on. Much information can be gleaned by listening to how you respond to superiors, peers and inmates. Does the employee cower to supervisors even when the situation deems otherwise? Is the employee on a good basis with peers? Does the employee seem to like or dislike inmates? Does the employee display professionalism with all groups, only a certain group, or at all? What better way to find out than to listen and have the employee tell them?

Listening is useful for the application of their tools (steps four through eleven). It is extremely necessary to know the employee's likes and dislikes. If the proposed victim hunts, the team will need to find an inmate hunter who speaks that particular sporting jargon and tells the accompanying stories. If the staff member appears religious or enthusiastic about such topics as nature or politics, conversation becomes styled around those topics in an attempt to form a close friendship. If the employee has a dislike, the team member—usually the turner—becomes knowledgeable on the subject and mirrors the employee's negative view, backed with many personal stories and facts.

Personal data such as home address, phone number, spouse's job, number of cars and the like prove valuable in helping to formulate a life style picture. Although each datum taken separately seems trivial, the accumulation says a lot. Inmates like to get this information when the employee does not pay attention to an inmate's presence and just talks—such as during a phone conversation or a discussion on the tier or in a hallway. Employees should always be aware of who is listening.

Verbal Observation

The previous observations, that of body language and listening, continue without the employee's involvement with the set-up team. But once preliminary theories and predictions

44

are established at the inmate "bull sessions," preliminary testing must begin. A turner will arrive on the scene with several friendly inmates who confirm the turner's validity and extol his virtues. The team needs to know how the employee gets along with the turner and thus the conversation begins. Does the employee accept him as more than an inmate? . . . enough to get overly friendly? He will like the things the employee likes, and dislike the things the employee dislikes. The turner's conversation is very calculated.

The team also needs to verify the employee's reaction to negative verbal interaction. In this process, the confinee engages an employee in conversation. He may make subtle allusions to rule infractions, tragic experiences, sex, or any subject that tends to mar a professional interaction. He very carefully monitors the individual's movements and facial expressions. He looks for signs of approval or disapproval. He wants to know if the conversation makes his victim feel uncomfortable, or if he can feed this person's ego. Jokes reflecting the sensual side of life, stories of sad experiences, and tales of injury situations provide gauges of how his victim feels on such matters.

When an inmate asks an employee for a favor, that person's response to the request will tell the manipulator a great deal about the person. In verbal observation, there may only be an expression that delivers a message from victim to manipulator . . . here the reaction is slight. On the other hand, the reaction can be strong, vehement, and prolonged. It shows force. Turners, other team members, or runners will explore these verbal response areas through conversation. Employees should be aware of the message the inmate is really getting in a conversation.

Action Observation

In verbal observation, the manipulator voices the suggestion of his intent to violate a rule to test the stand his victim will take. In action observation, he actually violates the rule to determine whether or not his bull session theory on the employee's reaction is correct. This action involves some risk on the inmate's part, but remember, the employee has been well observed, and the violation will be extremely minor at first. In verbal observation when the inmate made the suggestion of rules violation, he tentatively determined by his victim's reaction to the suggestion that the employee would allow the violation. However, he must be sure. In action observation, he actually violates the rule. To illustrate: Many institutions control housing area tier activity by permitting only the inmates living on a particular tier to be there. An inmate, who had been doing unsolicited favors for a housing officer, said to the employee, "I know I'm not allowed to be on your tier, but I need to talk to a friend so tomorrow you may notice I'm up there. However, I'll only be a few minutes." The officer said nothing because perhaps he felt an obligation to the inmate for the previous favors. The inmate surmised the violation would be tolerated and the next day he appeared on the tier. Again the officer said nothing, pretending not to notice the violation. The inmate's assumption had been correct. He created a condition that made rule enforcement difficult for the officer.

If the victim ignores the verbal suggestion to minor rule infraction and looks the other way, the inmate will act out the violation. Forms of action observation that deliver messages to inmates are: methods of command, responses to emergencies, levels of tolerance and satisfaction with the job. Team members create situations to see how a potential victim acts under those conditions.

When the initial observation phase is complete, a bank of knowledge has been acquired that determines selection of a victim. Once a consensus has been reached, the information is thoroughly discussed again at bull sessions and a course of action for implementation of complex manipulative processes plotted. Employees should be aware of the messages their actions deliver.

SELECTION OF A VICTIM

Victims of inmate manipulations are selected intentionally and accidentally. The team members have to expend a lot of time and energy to turn an employee, so selection constitutes an important step. Many employees have been selected and then tested against the team's personality profile of them. If the profile proves wrong, the team usually discards the employee as a victim and seeks a more gullible one.

Intentional Selection

When inmate observers notice an employee who appears extroverted, friendly and naive, a suspicion is born that presupposes a weakness in that individual. The assumption that these characteristics can be manipulated creates an intentional observation procedure to verify the suspicion. Although lack of experience and longevity on the job are not prerequisites for selection, statistically they prove helpful qualities. Inmates intentionally observe new employees who have not acquired an understanding of the prison environment for their susceptibility to the inmate wish.

Accidental Selection

An employee of experience or even a newcomer to corrections can very often display an impression of confidence, good judgment and strength. Team members shy away from people possessing these qualities because behavioral manipulation is difficult. Inmates also circumvent employees grouped into this category because the characteristics are firmly imbedded in the personality. Occasionally, manipulators inadvertently discover a weakness in one of these people and an accidental selection occurs.

In researching this phase of the set-up process, the authors discovered cases where victim selection occurred because of an employee's change in job assignment. For example, shortly after his probation period was completed, an officer was assigned to supervise an inmate work crew made up of felons who were about to be released on parole. The officer held this job for six years and in that time he had only been exposed to prisoners on their good behavior. His reassignment placed him in charge of a unit that housed hard core criminals who were masters at manipulation, and his six years' experience had not equipped him for this setting. By doing favors for him, inmates noticed he felt obligated, and soon he succumbed to their demand to reciprocate. He eventually brought in marijuana and, in time, lost his job.

Any trait possessed by an employee that inmates can construe as a weakness can result in that individual's selection as a victim of a set-up. To illustrate: In one institution an officer was engaged in conversation with an inmate on the main yard. While talking, the inmate kept trying to roll a cigarette, but a strong wind blew all of his tobacco away. Feeling sorry for the inmate, the officer gave him a cigarette from his package. As the conversation continued, he eventually gave the inmate another. When they concluded their talk, the officer gave the inmate the rest of the package and returned to his duties. The inmate receiving the cigarettes was grateful, but a nearby group of inmates observing the officer saw his act of kindness as a weakness. They observed him further, befriended him, tested him, and completed the set-up process.

This officer was a veteran of sixteen years' service. During his career, he had been approached by many inmates —some were very sophisticated and cunning—yet he never succumbed to their demands. So, one wonders, why this time? What was different?

It was later discovered that he had developed financial problems. He made the mistake of sharing these problems with inmates who had befriended him. Three hundred dollars had been placed in his lunch box just prior to the end of his shift. At home, he discovered the money and kept it. Inmates were now provided with a lever to use against him. Even if one feels a friendship between oneself and an inmate who is honest and true, other inmates detecting the relationship may, through pressure, coercement, and subtle set-up processes, attempt to cash in on it.

Inmates know that changes or anticipated changes (see Case Histories II and III) can tend to make a person more vulnerable to inmate attention. The change or anticipated change can be job related or family orientated and be of a positive or negative nature. In either case, emotions seem to be more at the surface and inmates scan for these signs.

Soft, Hard and Mellow

Inmate manipulators place correctional employees into three categories: soft, hard, and mellow. *Soft* employees are usually very trusting, overly-familiar and naive. They are understanding and sympathetic to inmate problems and have a strong desire to help those in need. These are not all bad qualities, but combined with the inability to say NO or take command of a situation, they produce a person susceptible to manipulation. *Hard* employees are those who go strictly by the rule book. They grant an inmate no leeway. *Mellow* employees are those who know when to be soft, when to be hard and how to use these traits at appropriate times. Inmates concentrate on the soft person and the hard person—the soft person because of the hesitancy to say NO or take command, and on the hard person because inmates feel the hardness disguises a weakness in the individual. Research has proven this assumption to be correct more often than not.

They leave the mellow person alone, not because that person cannot be manipulated but because the process would take too much time. The appropriateness of a mellow person's actions discourages the manipulative process.

In summation, inmates "peg" prison employees for what their attitudes and actions represent to them, and they are amazingly accurate in their final opinion.

TEST OF LIMITS AND FISH TESTING

Inmates develop a number of ideas and theories during the observation period. Assumptions are made about the employee's ability or inability to function under stress, one's level of tolerance, how effectively that person will take command, etc. These ideas and feelings about the victim are tested using two approaches.

The *test of limits* is a process of pushing, bending, breaking and circumventing minor rules to determine how far the manipulator can go before an employee takes action. *Fish testing* occurs when members of a set-up team request minor items that the employee is not supposed to issue. The request usually comes after team members have been particularly nice to the employee or made him or her feel obligated by doing volunteer work. The intent here is to determine how quickly, how easily, and how much an employee will give. In all the cases researched, it was found that team members and runners were used in both phases of the testing process.

Tests proceed at a quarter-step pace so as not to alert the victim. If an employee allows a great deal of license, the testing process is interspersed with support pledges to ward off suspicion of the proposed set-up. Inmates keep up the pressure because they believe that one out of every so many will succumb. This is especially true when manipulating a woman. Inmates are persistent.

Testing is a slow, subtle reading process that goes on

throughout the entire set-up. In preliminary verbal and action observation, testing was limited to minor kinds of things which led inmates to assume that given the proper set of circumstances their victim could be coerced into major violations. Now, the testing process becomes more serious and the tools of a set-up are put to work.

TOOLS OF A SET-UP

The Department of Corrections hires people for their good qualities, and employees should strive to maintain these. Consequently, they must guard against the inmates taking advantage of emotions that can be freely expressed in the free society. The tools utilized by inmates are the employees' own feelings and concerns. Team members allot their control of these tools according to the way they read the employees' sensitivities. Manipulators know just when to apply the different steps and when to back off.

The steps presented in this section follow the typical sequence of their appearance in the set-up process. However, they may proceed in any order, as they are calculated to validate another step's credence.

THE SUPPORT SYSTEM

A series of praises designed to befriend and develop a sense of togetherness and understanding sum up the inmate support system. This step begins subtly, then spirals using verbal and nonverbal approaches. Beginning verbal support could be side comments to another inmate about a staff decision, "That was sure a good idea!" The comments then become directly aimed at the staff member and gradually grow to be quite blatant, "You're the best cop in the joint." In the nonverbal support process, an astute manipulator will hopefully make himself indispensable. Again, it starts out cautiously such as always being on time; possibly being enthusiastic about the assignment, but definitely performing well; and in general, making the employee's job easier. In one case, an inmate clerk created a unique filing system that only he understood. On a day when he was ill, the office was difficult to manage without him. His highly efficient system operated only under his guidance. Staff immediately regained control by learning the system.

The inmate attempts to create a friendship which makes inmate requests for favors difficult to refuse. Manipulators want the employee to feel obligated. Support in a set-up situation can also be offers of help, promises of loyalty, agreeing with ideas and philosophies, and telling the victim that his or her approach to inmates is better than that of any other staff member. Pledges of devotion, faith in the individual, and complete trust also exemplify common approaches. The thrust of their actions tries to develop a strong trusting friendship, thus making the employee feel worthwhile and better than everyone else. An example of the support system follows.

Two inmates approached Officer Smith. "Good morning, Officer Smith. This is Inmate Jones. You know, the fellow I recommended to replace me when I go on parole."

"Oh, yes," Smith said, "how are you? I'm sorry I didn't remember, but I've had a lot on my mind."

"That's O.K., I understand," the prospective clerk said. "Is it O.K. if I work for you? My friend said you're the best officer in this whole system."

"Well, I try to be fair," Officer Smith said.

"Fair!" the former clerk exclaimed, turning to Inmate Jones. "Let me tell you how fair this man is. He doesn't write 'popcorn beefs' (disciplinary reports). He talks to people. This is probably the fairest man in the system, and because he's fair he's got an administrator on his back who likes to see inmates suffer. Oh, darn, I left my cigarettes in my room. Mr.

Smith, could you . . . "

Smith gave them each a cigarette and one for later.

"Wow, see what I mean?" the former clerk said to Inmate Jones. "That goddamn administrator wouldn't do this. He'd say, 'Suffer, Sucker'. This guy is the best officer in the joint and they treat him like he was one of us. Now you treat him right! He ain't like the rest of these cops."

"Well, thanks," Officer Smith said, "and you're right. They do kind of look down on me, but I don't see you guys as convicts—you're human beings. True, you've made a mistake, but you're paying for it, so why should I make your life more difficult?"

"That's great, and if Jones doesn't do a good job for you, I'll personally kick his ass," the inmate said.

"Oh, I'm sure he will," Smith continued. "If you recommended him, he's got to be O.K."

"One thing is for sure," the former clerk said, "We convicts won't treat you like some of these cops do . . . by the way, Jones, Officer Smith's wife is a fantastic baker, and," he continued jokingly, "I'll bet he forgot those cookies he was going to bring in . . . ."

This excerpt comes from an actual set-up case history and shows the effective use of the support system, and other set-up steps. The employee was made to feel he was something special, that his peers did not understand him, and that where he could not trust the people he worked for, he could count on the inmates.

The officer brought in the cookies which inmates later used as a lever against him. Their effort to coerce him into bringing in drugs paid off. Officer Smith complied out of fear of exposure and the possible loss of his job. Custody later apprehended him and terminated his employment.

EMPATHY AND/OR SYMPATHY

Inmates often try to do the right thing and in the process discover a staff member whose heart goes out to them. They covet this attention and will go to any length such as lying to maintain it. They may have no intention of victimizing the person, but only to obey the dictates of their conscience, which, at this point could be seen as an act of integrity. However, the realization and discovery of a highly emotional staff member can cause an inmate to seek favors if he senses an employee's deep emotional investment in his problems would make the request difficult to refuse. He acquires information about the person in order to empathize and create situations to elicit sympathy.

Empathy bases itself on a shared understanding, experience, or vicarious experience of feelings, thoughts, or attitudes. It draws forth the intellectual identification in these areas of one person with another: it forms a bond. It necessitates neither compassion nor pity—just the sameness of feeling. A hunter identifies with a hunter. A non-smoker understands a non-smoker—at least on that particular topic. They share a common experience even though they may not have acquired it at the same time or place. The more areas encompassed by empathy between two people, the greater the bond between them grows. Two people who think alike form a mutual respect because they see the good qualities in each other. Inmates know this and use this tool to say in essence to the employee: I'm just like you, but I made a mistake and was caught. But, really, we're just alike.

Sympathy, on the other hand, demonstrates a feeling without necessarily having had the experience that induced the emotion. Pity or compassion for another's troubles affirms the sympathetic feeling. Empathy and sympathy are close associates but with one or two major differences. In empathy,

54

one can understand and identify with a person's problems without feeling sorry for him. In sympathy, one cannot. In sympathy one can feel sorry without even understanding the problem. In this dialogue between two inmates: "You have three children and no wife, and I have three children and no wife. Raising three children from a jail cell is not an easy task to perform," their similar circumstances show they share a level of understanding unique to the two of them. They have empathy for one another. They do not have to sympathize with each other, but it would be easy to do so.

An inmate manipulator will empathize on a nonpersonal level first, just sharing common experiences: "You should have heard this minister talk," or "You should have seen the antlers on that deer!" He will later try to get the employee to empathize with him on a more personal level, eventually to the point of sharing personal problems. Oddly, the inmate's likes, dislikes, and problems resemble those of his intended victim. He establishes a "you/me" situation—a ground of common, personal experiences trying eventually to evoke sympathy. Acquiring a lever on the employee may be attempted when his or her sympathetic feelings toward an inmate reach a peak.

The reader may recall that during the observation process, inmates gathered information about their victim's habits, hobbies, likes and dislikes—does this employee hunt, fish, like children, act religious and so forth. This information can now be drawn upon to empathize with the victim. The inmate grapevine, another source to gather empathy material, produces more information. For example, fifteen minutes after sharing with a fellow employee that his wife was having twins, the expectant father received a similar announcement of anticipating twins from an inmate whose wife was in a family way. This later proved untrue, but the inmate and the officer shared great empathy for a period of time.

Setting someone up by the use of empathy and/or sympathy is very effective. Consider this actual example.

An inmate, who had become involved in a correctional officer's problems through the use of empathy, discovered the man's vulnerable spot: his mentally retarded child whom he dearly loved. The inmate intimated to the officer that he, too, had such a child, but that his child always suffered poor health. Having learned during the observation phase of his set-up that this officer was a man of profound emotion, the prisoner maintained a daily commentary on the progressively worsening condition of his child. "Unless little Joey gets a certain type of treatment that I cannot afford, he will die," the inmate told the officer.

Because the officer understood the problems of raising such a youngster and felt sorry for little Joey and his father, he aided the inmate in an escape so he could see the child one more time before he passed away. The inmate lived close by and promised the staff member he would return before the morning count. "After all," the confined man said, "if you're kind enough to let a father hold his child one last time, there's no way I will let you down." Needless to say, the inmate never returned.

Empathy and sympathy remain very common and necessary tools of a set-up. Inmates applying these tools on a staff member will first find a level of understanding that they and the employee can identify with. They then seek sympathy from this person to gain entry into his or her deeper emotions. Inmates schooled in street psychology know that a person extends liberties more easily to someone when they have shared feelings on a profound personal level than when a person maintains anonymity on such issues.

THE PLEA FOR HELP

In this phase of the set-up process, inmates bank on the employee's need for ego fulfillment and closure. Employees want to know they perform well in a worthwhile job and like to see the results. A carpenter can build a chair and admire his completed product, but correctional employees never see the successful completion of their work. They daily view their failures. Most correctional employees strive to help the inmate return to society as a good citizen. If they succeed, the person is never seen again, but they do meet the recidivists.

Prison employees, like anyone else, need to know their services have value. Because they rarely run into the positive result of their efforts, they are highly susceptible to the plea for help. "A friend in need is a friend indeed," and inmates use and believe in this cliche. A friend will help another friend build a new life. Personal satisfaction and the feeling of a job well done bring the rewards. An inmate who has expressed faith in an employee will confess that he has been a failure all his life, that he lacks confidence, and he wishes to change his life style. He will discuss family, religion, money, and elicit sympathy for a life gone awry. "You," he will say, "and your unique abilities are the only things that will rehabilitate me. I need your help."

This is a delicate situation to handle. A sincere inmate must be helped: it is part of a correctional employee's job. How, then, can one be assured that an inmate is making an honest request as opposed to setting someone up? The truth is no one can be assured. But what an employee can do is try to check it out—in essence, test the inmate. The way to do this is to discuss the problem with someone else and *make sure the inmate knows that another employee is aware of the request.*

Keep everything out in the open! People who try to deceive a person do not want this openness. They must be careful what they do and say lest a more experienced employee detects the deception.

Beware of confidentiality! Prisoners who attempt to establish a you/me situation will tell staff members of a problem facing them that must be kept secret. Remember, there is nothing so secret that it cannot be shared with someone else. It is important to share and let the inmate know the information was passed on. If the request for confidentiality is sincere, the inmate will welcome aid from counselors, the chaplain, etc.—two minds are better than one. If the employee is being set-up, the manipulator, when he becomes aware his information has been shared, will find some way of letting his prospective victim know the situation has been resolved. And he may go in search of another victim.

Sample reply to a real plea for help: "Gee, Mr. Jones, thanks a lot for talking it over with the other counselor. What did he say? Maybe I could talk to him, too."

Sample reply from a set-up plea for help: "Gee, Mr. Jones, thanks a lot for talking it over with the other counselor. But last night, me and my buddies stayed up till three o'clock discussing it and we got it all taken care of. I sure do thank you for your concern, though."

Neither sample reply guarantees which is which, but, along with other signs, it offers a good indication.

The employee should be aware that an inmate, during a highly emotional crisis or an emergency situation, will take the opportunity to try and get a lever on the staff member in his plea for help. The inmate will have a real or feigned tragic event in his life and, based on sympathy and friendship, ask his victim to violate a rule. The employee will be assured that the violation is of crucial necessity and that it will be on a "one-time-only" basis. By using the previously discussed techniques, the inmate knows that the staff member will have a difficult time refusing because the team has already discovered the employee's vulnerable spots. The original support, empathy and sympathy given the employee has expanded into a two-way street. The inmate knows that the employee now has feelings for him. His investment of those tools will hopefully pay off.

An employee's job is to help inmates, and even though the heart may go out to all the difficult circumstances an inmate may be in, the employee must help the inmate in the prescribed manner using appropriate methods or channels.

THE WE/THEY SYNDROME

Recently, a prison staff member attended an after-work-hours party. Imbibing a bit too much, his conduct reached the realm of questionable demeanor. The following day, contacts overheard employees discussing the man's behavior, using expressions like "stupid, lacking in good judgment, and an alcoholic problem." Quite soon, team members not only reported the derogatory comments to the employee, but also revealed the identity of the staff talkers. Then the inmates said, "But they're wrong about you: they don't know you like we do. We know those things are not the real you. We don't feel that way. They are treating you just like they treat us." Hence the effective use of the we/they syndrome. The team wants to separate the victim from other staff so the victim will turn to inmates for ego support, etc. They want the employee to think: I'm O.K., you're O.K.–they're not O.K.

The controversial staff member took the bait and was caught in their net. He remarked to the inmates, "The 'sons of bitches' talk about me all the time. Other people do the same thing, why don't they talk about them?"

This situation provided the inmates with the foundation for a set-up which eventually culminated in the staff person bringing in whiskey and later begin escorted off the premises.

We/they situations demonstrate perhaps the most subtle of the set-up steps and always pit one staff member against another. Inmates want their proposed victim to identify with the "we" (victim and supportive inmates) and disassociate with the "they" (any staff—nonsupportive, neutral or even supportive). If a manipulator feels the support system does not work with his victim, he will attack other staff members to the person he is setting up in an effort to divide and conquer. Dissension among the rank works. For example, an inmate told a female victim that other women working in her area claimed she was inefficient. Hearing this, the woman became angry and no longer associated with those staff members. Having successfully pulled their victim away from her friends, inmates had more time and greater freedom to work on her. No one can deny that dissension occurs among staff. But the problems should remain at the staff level and be devoid of inmate involvement.

Another approach using the we/they syndrome is to dwell on a cause, racism or hate as a pulling away device. Inmates will support whatever position a susceptible employee advocates. For an illustration of this, read Case History II. The use of the same ethnic background, same neighborhood background, or same circumstance background puts pressure on the employee: "You're a brother who's up, I'm a brother who's down. As a brother (or sister) it's your obligation to help me more than you help others not in 'our group'." Obviously, all inmates deserve fair and equal treatment, and employees must not fall into the we/they trap.

Convicts want to pull the victim away from supervision interaction also. Manipulators count on the usual response when an intended victim reports suspicious behavior to supervisors. When advisors remark, "This is a prison, you have to expect that sort of thing. These people aren't in here for missing Sunday School, ya know," and, "If you can't stand the

60

heat, stay out of the kitchen," the employee feels betrayed. This person resolves never to report this type of behavior again out of fear the supervisor will feel he or she is unable to do the job.

OFFER OF PROTECTION

Consider the following conversation of an inmate and staff member.

Inmate: (1) With the amount of writing you have to do, you should have a Selectric typewriter.

(2) I'm surprised they don't give you one.

(3) After all, your material goes throughout the entire state, and as a representative of corrections, your stuff should look as professional as you appear to be.

Staff
Member: (4) I know, you're right, I put in a request for one, but they always come up with these lame excuses as to why they don't give me one.

Inmate: (5) They do the same thing to us.

(6) Tell you what.

(7) Let me have the next important thing you need done and done right.

(8) I know an inmate who works in an office where they have a Selectric and I'll have it done for you.

(9) You got that coming.

(10) You treat us prisoners like human beings—not numbers.

(11) You seem to understand that we are paying for our mistakes, and that we're here *as* punishment, not *for* punishment.

(12) If anyone says anything, I'll just tell them I took it upon myself to do this.

(13) I won't even mention your name.

Staff

Member: (14) Well, I don't want you to get in trouble, but...
O.K.

Inmate: (15) Trouble?! Me? What are they going to do, take away my driver's license?

This conversation actually took place with the intent to further the set-up process. Conversations like this often take place in corrections, and most of the time, the inmate is sincere. But what happens when he is not? What if he uses the situation as a foundation for a set-up? To analyze this, assume that you are the person with whom the inmate is conferring. See how many steps to a set-up you can identify.

Remember, he has observed you. He knows your limitations. He has already toyed with your emotions. In short, he knows you quite well. Also, the fact that he felt free enough to suggest or imply that you would buy into something a little on the dishonest side shows he has done his homework.

When the conversation began, you will notice that sentences one and two in the first paragraph make the subtle suggestion that you are not being treated properly by the people you work for—a touch of the we/they syndrome.

Sentence three brings in the support system. It is designed to compliment, build your ego, and make you feel a little disgusted because your talents are not given the importance they deserve.

Sentence four shows the staff member is taking the bait and talks about "they" derogatorily.

Sentence five uses the we/they syndrome as the seed-thoughts that will eventually turn his victim.

Sentences six, seven and eight go back to the support system. The inmate is doing you a favor. And, again comes the subtle suggestion that you are not being dealt with fairly by your peers. The inmate also emits a touch of sympathy for your situation.

Sentence nine, "You got that coming," is a way of say-ing inmates like you as a friend, and they will not treat you as badly as the people you work for or with treat you—a bit stronger we/they application.

Sentences ten and eleven utilize the support system, the we/they syndrome and establish empathy. It sets you apart from your fellow employees, preys on your emotions, and builds your ego.

Sentences twelve and thirteen use the support system, the we/they syndrome, and have the subtle inclusion of an offer of protection. The inmate is willing to take the blame for something you allow him to do. There is another very in-teresting trap here: In sentence fourteen you accepted the in-mate's offer. He has learned by the test of limits that you will "look the other way" to improve job performance—a trait you see as a strength and he sees as a weakness. In this example the offer of protection is barely noticeable, but it is neverthe-less there. Sentence fifteen implies that the inmate can afford to get in trouble whereas the employee cannot. The inmate indicates that "taking the heat" does not bother him and that he is protecting the employee from any reprimand.

A more graphic example of an offer of protection can be found in situations where the offer is presented after in-stilling a feeling of fear. In an area where an enclosure exists, inmates point out to the victims how easy it would be for someone to force them into the forbidden spot and possibly harm or kill them. Rapid assurance that they will not let that happen to the employee addressed, rounds out the conversa-tion. The victim is usually grateful for the concern and shows signs of willingness to become more friendly than before.

If the employee appears not to be overly concerned by this fear information, the inmates then stage an event that dramatically demonstrates a need for inmate friendship and protection. This occurs when no other staff can witness the incident or assist the victim. Usually paid runners pose as assailants, and team members come to the rescue if the employee requires aid.

The planned crisis is not designed to cause injury, but only to deepen the employee's concern about safety. Turners want victims to be grateful and feel a real need for their presence. They want the employee to think that peers may not be able to stop harm, but that the inmates will not let another incident happen because the victim has an "in" with the inmates. As the friendship between the victim and the protectors becomes stronger, inmates feel free to take greater license with the individual. Allusions to sex and a touch system appear on the scene to give the outward appearance of an even stronger bond.

ALLUSIONS TO SEX

The manipulation of human behavior is an extremely complex procedure. Its psychological processes alone require years of study. Yet, there seems to be inherent in mankind an ability to gain from his fellowman by preying on his emotions, to add to or take from his pleasures, to increase and decrease body tissue needs, or to distort facts and information. From childhood, we learn to manipulate our parents, later our brothers and sisters, then our acquaintances. But the greatest manipulation occurs between men and women, particularly when the motivation is sex.

Some people devise techniques for gratification that even though rejected, may not necessarily be offensive. Conversely, some others develop methods in order to satiate this drive that are devious, forced, and have criminal intent. Controlling the urge for sex in the prison community is now, and always has been one of correction's greatest problems. The inability to control the sex drive results in homosexual relationships and forcible rape. The central concentration in these cases is usually from one prisoner to another, and when one aggressor manipulates another prisoner for sex, the methods are direct and swift. But quite frequently, the prisoner directs attention to a staff member.

When a prisoner manipulates a female staff member for sex, conditions and situations must be carefully planned and implemented so as not to create suspicion while the inmate maneuvers her into position for the demand. The turner who initiates the ploy develops an overly-familiar friendship with the female victim. The con-wise prisoner creates an image of himself that directly opposes someone seeking sex on an animal level or even seeking it at all: the victim develops a trust and naiveté that leaves her vulnerable to proposition first, insistence second, and finally, force.

In set-up situations where the proposed victim is a female employee, the prisoner makes allusions to sex at any point in the set-up process where he feels their friendship will tolerate such references. In the early stages, the prisoner directs his allusions to sex toward the employee but away from himself. For example: In a recent case a prisoner said to a female correctional officer with whom he had established a friendship, "Last night while four of us guys were playing cards, one guy said if there was only you and him in the housing unit, you would freely have sex with him. I put him in his place, though. I told him you were not like that, and to stop talking that way." The reference was directed away from the manipulator. Having made the statement, the prisoner promptly assures the victim that he put the over-inquisitive fellow in his place. The design of the allusion places the employee's anger, if any, away from the person revealing the conversation.

The originator of the statement finds great importance in how the employee responds to the information because it determines the next step in the set-up process. If she makes no comment at all, he assumes a freedom to make further allusions to sex. If her comment denotes a philosophical approach such as, "When a man is in confinement, comments like that are common and expected," the inmate assumes the woman has a basic understanding of the needs of men in confinement and he feels safe in continuing the process. If her response requests further details, the inmate formulates the opinion that she anxiously advocates further discussion on sexual matters. But, if her response is cold and indifferent, such as: "I need that inmate's name and number so I can report him to my supervisor, and, if what you say is true, I will also arrange your work hours so that you are only here during the time the others are present. I do not appreciate talk like that, nor do I appreciate hearing about it!", her reaction will have the effect of closing the subject. Depending on how much inmates have invested in this set-up process, her response can also conclude further attempts at manipulation. In cases where the inmate sees the victim as responding in a positive manner, his allusions to sex will eventually be directed less and less "out there", and more and more toward himself as the person in need of attention.

Institutions where female employees are exposed to inmates on a one-to-one basis should take a serious look at the procedure. Any inmate assigned to work with a woman under these conditions, even a convict with good intentions, will eventually receive pressure from his peers. They will make statements like, "We know you don't just talk during that hour the two of you are alone. What's going on?" An inmate gains respect and status from the prison population if it is thought that he has successfully compromised an employee. The pressure to confide an intimate situation becomes greater than he can handle. Thus, the inmate ultimately confesses to the false rumor.

Employees knowing that a female works alone with an inmate for long periods of time have also started rumors. Statements like, "I wonder what's going on in there?", develop into, "Something *is* going on in there!" As the suspicion transfers from one employee to another, it gains in distortion and force, and has resulted in some employees resigning from their jobs. This kind of exposure is unfair to the employee and in one case resulted in a divorce. The woman's husband, also an institution employee, allowed his emotions to build on an untrue rumor that his wife provided sexual favors to an inmate. He could not rid himself of the feeling that rumors have some foundation in truth or they do not start. Arguments developed between the two of them until separation became inevitable.

Allusions to sex extend to male employees also in the form of a dirty joke, a pornographic story, a "girly" magazine, etc. The intent is to communicate on a nonprofessional level, form a common bond, and perhaps even get the employee to relate some personal information. Rarely do inmates pressure male staff members for homosexual acts; however, it has been known to happen.

Because the majority of penal institutions house male felons, the authors addressed most issues from that standpoint. But the same set-up process occurs in a penal institution for women. Allusions to sex are designed to use sex as a coercement or lever on a male employee in order to get him to bring in contraband. If a male staff member values job security, he must keep his personal life out of the institution, (See Case History V).

THE TOUCH SYSTEM

Inmates create touching situations with both male and female employees, but more so with females. Touching of male employees usually consists of hand shaking, pats on the back, or placing one's hand on the shoulder to form a closer bond.

The touching of females must be less obvious with greater caution exercised. This usually begins with the flicking of a dirt speck from the woman's clothing, or the straightening of a coat or blouse collar. It progresses to touching her shoulders in an attempt to pass by. The touching grows more and more frequent and more and more prolonged in a well-timed procedure usually accomplished when the inmate and staff member are alone. If the staff member registers no complaints to the prolonged hands-on process, an accident occurs. The inmate trips, and in the attempt to regain footing, touches the female's breast. It has long been known that even an accidental touching of the breast increases a personal bond. He apologizes profusely, and the incident, it seems, is forgotten. However, the team closely observes her for signs of approval or disapproval. Also, a period of time is allowed to pass to see if she reports the incident to her supervisors. If not, the touching gets more serious.

If a set-up victim develops a curious expression indicating doubt of the validity of any phase in the process, inmates fortify themselves with stories designed to gain back the employee's sympathy, thus taking the victim's mind off any previous skepticism. Attention is directed towards the inmate's problem instead of the employee's self concern. If enough victim sympathy can be elicited, the inmate hopes to get back to the touch system by getting a sympathetic hug.

THE RUMOR CLINIC

An adverse rumor that is completely untrue could be started about anyone reading this book. Friends who have known you all your life would be quick to say, "I don't believe it!" But they will walk away with that "gut level feeling" that the rumor must have some validity or it would not have been generated. A common human frailty is transferring this type of information, and inmates use this trait to its fullest extent.

In the previously discussed we/they syndrome, inmates began pulling their victim away from staff by creating situations where one employee becomes irritated with the others. If the set-up team has succeeded in pulling the victim away from other staff—peers and supervisors—the isolation process must come full cycle. Staff must be pulled away from the victim. The rumor clinic completes the process of effectively detaching a staff member from peers.

A well-placed rumor will create doubt in the minds of everyone, even the people who openly profess disbelief, and the street psychologist takes full advantage of this human tendency. The team members plant seed-thoughts that lead to the breakdown of professionalism among the gossips—staff and inmates alike. They begin the rumors in an area of the facility that is away from the victim's work area. For one reason, the distance tends to take the blame away from the team members. For another, it allows the rumor to gain force as it makes its way to the victim's work area. Peer attitudes toward the victim begin changing as the force of the rumor intensifies, and contacts with the individual become less and less frequent. People like to go with a winner: a bad rumor, true or not, makes the staff member a loser. The employee whom the rumors are about feels isolated, which provides members of the set-up team the opportunity of strengthening their bonds of friendship. "We don't believe the rumors," they staunchly say, and, "They are treating you just like they treat us!" Inmates are the victim's only "friends." This phase of the set-up also produces an ideal situation to introduce or reemphasize the offer of protection.

Inmates in one correctional institution began spreading a rumor that a certain officer was taking state supplies home in his lunch box. Because the officer had a spotless reputation for honesty, staff members claimed they did not believe it. As the rumor accelerated in force, staff attitudes began changing and one evening the officer was challenged at the main gate and searched. Nothing was found. The officer was unable to face his peers in the days that followed because of the "Where there's smoke, there's fire" attitude and he went in search of other employment.

TURNOUTS

A "jailhouse turnout" in prison jargon refers to an inmate selected by his peers to function as a male prostitute, then forced into submission against his will. The term "turnout" also refers to employees of a correctional facility who have been successfully coerced into supplying prisoners with illegal contraband or illicit favors. The turnout phase of a set-up is the point where provocateurs make their wants known. It is—a point of no return. Up until now, inmates violated no laws or institution rules. They applied eleven of the set-up steps without being detected, and even if the plot had been discovered, their chicanery would go unpunished.

But in this last process things are different: turning a person out cannot be accomplished without breaking the law. Before taking this step, deceptors must be confident the set-up has been properly administered and the person being deceived can be controlled. These next three steps—the turnout process—are designed to give that assurance of inmate control and ultimate success. Like a cat stalking a mouse, manipulators spring! But not with physical force; that comes later. Psychological pressure pounces first. A cat toys with a mouse, letting it free, then catching it again. Deceivers use the same trickery.

Employees, unaware of the set-up pattern, do not realize

that the seemingly unrelated incidents from different, perhaps segregated areas of a facility, are really well coordinated through the inmate grapevine. The length of a set-up varies according to the time allowed (is the employee there only on a short assignment, or is there no time limit?) and to how the employees react (how gullible or susceptible are they with their feelings and concerns?). If an employee has not been rejected as a candidate for a set-up sometime during the eleven steps, this person faces real trouble.

Prisoners are going to make their demands and expose their true intention. What has seemed in the past to be friendly, innocent and helpful, now becomes serious. If the victim refuses to turn into a "pack horse" because of the psychological pressure, inmates apply their skills of control by force. The ultimate turnout step is quick, dangerous and final; and the claws of the stalker are fully extended.

THE SHOPPING LIST

Acquiring contraband brings home one reason the inmates conceived the set-up in the first place. Everything that transpired was leading to this point. The testing, the support, the friendship, concern—all zeroed in to their calculated intent: to make an urgent, though polite request for prohibited goods based on what seems to be a valid need. Inmates initially solicit contraband on a one-time-only basis, and it only becomes a demand if the victim refuses their polite request. The reader must realize that the victim responded so well to all phases of the set-up that manipulators now feel comfortable in asking for the contraband. They created a condition where refusal is difficult, to say the least.

The shopping list demands for male employees consist usually of drugs, alcohol, money, and weapons, respectively, and on a few occasions, homosexual acts. For female victims, the request is almost always for sex first, and then drugs, al-

71

cohol, or money.

The shopping list exposes the set-up. Once the victim hears the request, the employee now knows he or she has been compromised. The initial reaction usually produces shock or disbelief—not a good frame of mind in which to make a quick decision. Inmates know they risk disciplinary action for the request, so for the inmates involved, backing out is never considered. Their coercion begins with a sales pitch interspersed with reasons for the need and justifications for the act—all calculated to assuage the victim's mind. (See Case History II).

THE LEVER

A lever will lift, pry, or force an object to respond through the proper distribution of pressure, and herein lies the back-up point of the entire set-up process. If the manipulator has done his job properly, the right distribution of pressure has been applied and now he gets into position to make his demand. He acquired a lever, and the device is going to force a prison employee into breaking the law. A lever can be obtained anywhere during the first eleven steps of the set-up. Once acquired, it remains in abeyance until inmates announce their demand to the victim. If the employee meets the shopping list demand, the lever is never mentioned. But if the employee refuses, the manipulator sternly reminds the victim of the earlier indiscretion (the lever) and threatens exposure if compliance is not forthcoming. In essence he says, "The fun is over, the law violated. If caught, I'm in trouble, refuse and so are you." The situation at this point could be very volatile and dangerous. If the use of coercion, demands, and fear do not produce the items demanded, manipulators will not hesitate to use the ultimate force. Employees who meet the demand are usually reassured that no further requests will be made of them: compliance means freedom. This ploy makes the employees feel pressure will be lifted when the request is fulfilled. As inmates place additional pressures on the victim, a personality change in the victim becomes obvious. The employee becomes abnormally quiet, socializes less and less with peers, and develops a worried expression. The job becomes a great burden, and reporting to work each day remains an effort. It is only a matter of time before total exposure of the episode explodes.

In the case to follow, the request and demand of a shopping list, and the creation and use of a lever are clearly shown.

Officer Fredricks was a man of extraordinary loquacity. His constant running conversations were largely ignored until an inmate observer began noticing Fredricks grew even more talkative when prisoners living in his unit approached him with their personal problems. The inmate surmised that the officer's loquaciousness was a shield masking emotions the man had difficulty controlling. Credence for this theory gained confirmation when the inmate observer witnessed Fredricks granting favors to emotionally charged prisoners because he felt sorry for them. On the basis of these observations, inmates selected him as a victim for manipulation. A team formed and established a system of praise and pleas for help. And when a rumor developed suggesting that Fredricks had been stealing state equipment for use in his home, they protected his reputation. A testing situation occurred when the chosen turner, whose wife had just passed away, asked Fredricks to hide a sympathy card addressed to the deceased woman's parents in his lunch box and mail it when he got to town. There was nothing wrong with the card so he mailed it (creation of a lever). Inmates continued their praise and especially complimented Fredricks for mailing the card they had all signed. This small act gave a great deal of comfort to the inmate husband of the deceased.

Some time later, the inmate widower developed a cold.

The hospital medication did not seem to work so he said to the officer, "My eyes water from this cold and I can't study for school. My grades are not too good, and if I flunk, I won't get my parole. Then I won't be able to care for my kids, because I'll be stuck here. A Vicks inhaler would stop the congestion, and the inmate store doesn't sell them. I will never ask for another thing, but being with my kids is important to me." Fredricks, being a family man, understood the importance of children having a father, especially since the mother had recently passed away. It cost only 89 cents, so why not? (Creation of a second lever.)

The following day, his inmate friends approached and told him a package containing marijuana would be dropped at his home and he had to smuggle it into the institution for them. At first, he refused until the inmate widower stepped forward and said, "Look, sucker, you ain't got no choice! I got the Vicks inhaler you brought in and evidence showing you took a letter out for me. I got your job! Now, if you don't do as you're told, we're going to kill you. You're as good as dead!"

Fredricks was caught bringing in the marijuana and his employment terminated. The investigation that followed showed the inmate's wife had not died and he had no children.

In the aforementioned case of Officer Fredricks, the officer knew the inmates had "something" on him, but since it generated out of a friendly, concerned gesture, he erroneously did not believe they would hold it over his head. In the next case, because of his lack of consistency and lack of control, the officer did not even know the inmates had a lever on him.

Inmates first took notice of this officer when he disciplined one inmate for not cleaning his room, but permitted his orderly to leave his living quarters unattended. This inconsistency in the enforcement of rules told inmates that, given proper conditions, the officer would circumvent institution regulations. A team of inmates not assigned to his area volunteered to work for him stating they just wanted to keep busy. They worked hard, did an excellent job, and cultivated the officer's friendship. They even got themselves transferred into his area. They knew the officer would find it hard to say NO when small, seemingly unimportant rules were violated, such as allowing their friends into his area who had no business being there.

The set-up team employed runners to act unruly in his area. The officer allowed and was grateful for his "helpers'" control of the disruptive situation. The officer and his select inmate friends formed a closer bond. As the minor disturbances continued, his inmates told him they intended to keep trouble-makers in line to make living conditions more tolerable by just pushing a guy around a little. The officer "looked the other way." Actually, the inmate victim was badly beaten, then raped by six people.

Soon, the inmates requested a gun. The officer turned them in, but it was too late. The lever they had acquired involved forceable rape and there were no officer reports. When the officer reported the gun episode, a large number of inmates exposed him, saying he knew of the rape case all along. The evidence presented against him caused his termination of employment.

Most employees realize that helping inmates rehabilitate and showing compassion is of primary importance in their job, but they must conduct their actions through the appropriate channels provided by the department. The act that produces a lever is usually known by the employees, but they place little consequence on it because they feel it demonstrates a humanitarian gesture. The inmates count on this naivete: if the employees expose their own indiscretions, the inmates lose their lever and thus their use of the victim. The inmates still stand on safe ground, though, because the manipulators have not as yet violated an institution rule—at least not up to step eleven.

Presentation of the shopping list (asking for or accepting any gift of money, property, material or substance from institution employees) makes the askers vulnerable to disciplinary action. The use of the lever (to gain favors by use of threat) presents another risk of disciplinary action, and the inmates are further committed to carry the set-up to its conclusion. They prepare themselves to use any means at their disposal to get their way—even the ultimate force.

THE STING

The look of nettles seems quite innocent; as a matter of fact, the plant appears very attractive. Yet come in contact with it, and its sting feels most uncomfortable. A set-up is similar to nettles with one major difference—its sting can be lethal. The sting wraps up all the steps in the set-up. The victim has undergone all the courting steps, a lever has been established and the shopping list presented. The victim must now decide to "Do as you are told or you will be harmed." No one wants to be hurt, and most inmates involved in a set-up would rather not resort to the use of force, but as a last resort one can rest assured they will. The final sting has caused some employees to resign, leave their jobs in disgrace, and others to die.

Two of the most basic life problems are linked to the individual's power position vis à vis his fellow man: (1) to make others fulfill one's own wishes, and (2) the fear of being controlled by others with the consequent loss of autonomy that is believed to be fundamental to the conception of the self. These opposites are incongruously exaggerated in the paranoid thinking and causes the creation of diabolical schemes.

76

Inmate manipulators have a dream wish for omnipotence. They fear the loss of the self through its capture by another. Their entire set-up procedure aims to achieve dominance. To assure ultimate success, force or threatened force injects the final sting.

If the victim succumbs to the threatened use of the lever or the threatened use of force and brings in contraband or performs illicit favors, the inmates have won the battle of the minds. They possess the will of their victim. For some reason, it appears that the team still lacks satisfaction; after the "mule" has performed over a period of time, the inmates cause the exposure of the employee's indiscretion if authorities have not yet caught him or her in the act.

When the set-up reaches the last stage, most employees comply with the demand. Many resign. Some take the risk of being injured or embarrassed when the lever is introduced and expose the involved inmates. This is a high risk situation and the rewards range from small to nil.

For a correctional officer who brought whiskey into his institution, the sting was termination of his employment.

For a supervising cook who refused to bring in drugs, the sting was to be death by boiling in a 150 gallon steam vat. He was saved by correctional officers who rushed into the kitchen after hearing a scuffle.

For a female employee, who had taken out letters and brought in small contraband, ultimate force was used. Even after inmates threatened the use of their levers, she refused their demands for sexual favors. Her sting? Death.

Downing
a
Duck
(An Inmate's Version)

This story was related by prisoners who know and understand the set-up process. They were inmates who, at one time or another, had been implicated as conspirators in several illegal contraband cases involving prison staff members. They would not discuss their own individual techniques of modifying prison personnel behavior, but they did relate events of a set-up implemented by one of their cohorts, citing the procedure as typical. The authors cannot attest to the validity of their statements; however, the file of the individual being discussed does indicate consistency between his behavior in the situation and the expected manipulative pattern.

The prison jargon term "duck" refers to an institution employee who can be manipulated or easily fooled.

Cracking the Shell Takes Time and Effort

You have to go about developing a duck in a manner that creates very little suspicion. A man would be a fool to

78

just walk up to a joint cop and ask him or her to bring in "grass," booze or money. You have to go slow, which takes time and effort. The dudes who get caught are the ones who get over-anxious and move too fast. The first thing you gotta do is watch. You know, things like the way a person acts, walks, stands, sits, or dresses can tell you a hell of a lot about them. Things they laugh or smile at; what makes them sad or angry; their likes and dislikes; this is all important information if you really want to develop a duck. You gotta start small if you want to get a person to a point where they'll do just about anything you say. The last duck I developed was a natural. Naive, shy, friendly as hell, a do-gooder who could be made to believe anything. You see, prisons don't know how to warn their people. They gotta say, "Be friendly, be nice," but they don't know how to tell them when they're going overboard. So I'm gonna tell this story like he was my duck. At any rate I started my duck with nothing more than getting him to give me pencils and paper in excess of what he was supposed to give. Here's how I developed him.

Developing the Duck

I watched this cop for a long time. He had all the traits. He was uneasy around his boss, pushed the nice guy bit so strong on us he overlooked violation of some small unit rules; in other words, he didn't take care of business. He couldn't put across his orders with any kind of firmness, and the cons were givin' him a rough row to hoe. When you find a guy like this, you can pretty well figure you got a duck—but you can't be too hasty, you gotta be sure.

I sent some friends of mine to get him involved in a philosophical discussion to find out where his head was and to push him a little to see how far he'd let things go. They talked about how bad other cops treated them and how they hoped he didn't become like all other cops. He agreed, and told them about things he'd seen the other "bulls" do that supported their reason for disliking cops. While the talk was going on, some of the guys broke rules like stepping inside another con's cell, putting marks on the wall, suggesting playing poker—all minor rules violations. The officer said nothing. Each time he started to leave and tell some guy to knock it off they'd praise the hell out of him and he'd get back into the conversation. Me, I just watched. The guy was very easily distracted and we built on the nice guy image. He didn't look like a cop—sloppy dresser, half done jobs and he'd come unglued if someone said he did a poor job, or if someone didn't particularly like him. When this happened he'd get in "downer" conversations telling the cons how no one understood him. They'd agree, and build his ego. They got him on a first name basis—it's harder to tell a guy "NO" when you're that friendly.

When I was absolutely certain this guy was the one I wanted to develop, I had his unit orderlies do a sloppy job so he wouldn't pass inspection. The sergeant gave him hell. When the sarg left, I went over to the guy and said, "You know what, Pete, you didn't have that coming. The sarg doesn't know you like we do. Out of all the cops in this joint, you're the only one the cons trust. Remember, we told you where to find the convict home brew. He didn't remember you made that bust. I've been talking with the other cons in this wing and we're going to make you look good from now on." My duck kept raving on how that sergeant has been on his back; that he just can't seem to do anything right. So, I told him, "I got some extra time each day and I'll fix this place so you'll not only pass inspection, but you'll get a commendation for the cleanest wing in the joint. I ain't gonna let no crummy sergeants talk to you that way anymore." The cop said he would be grateful.

As the days and weeks passed, I worked my tail off for this joker. He began passing his inspections with honors. He had the habit of leaving his lunch box open or his cigarettes laying on his desk so I began helping myself. I didn't over do it, and he said nothing, so I asked him for a couple of full writing pads and a few new pencils. He was supposed to give only one pencil, usually used, and only a couple of sheets of paper. With a long explanation and unsteady voice he turned me down. Saying "No" was hard for him. I looked hurt and said, "Oh, I'm sorry, I wasn't thinking. I thought you knew I liked to relax and write after working at my regular job, then cleaning this unit for you. I only asked you because most of the guys in the wing told me you understood things like that —that you like to see us doing constructive things. Oh, well, it ain't no big thing." I tried to let my expression say my feelings were hurt, I was sorry he didn't trust me, and I guess he was like all other cops. With my head down I sauntered to my room. Shortly Pete was at my cell door. He made sure no one was looking then slid a dozen new pencils and three new writing tablets under my door. I said, "Pete!, you're the greatest! Just like all the guys say, you really try and help convicts stay out of trouble." I worked extra hard that next week winning Pete praise from the sergeant who formerly cussed him out. Pete was pleased and said, "Thank you, Terry." He used my first name, a sign I was developing him properly.

Several months had passed now and we had become good friends. I sought personal, financial, and marital advice, which he freely gave. And since he liked baseball, I liked baseball. He disliked hunting, so I disliked hunting. Now you gotta be careful with this, too. If you have too much in common, that's not good, so you let him talk you into believing as he does. For example, he asked me if I believed in God. I seemed hesitant and confused. I let him convince me there was a God. You gotta remember when developing a duck that you're always the student and he's the teacher. You appear

81

to be fascinated by his knowledge. You make him think you need his help; that he's making you a better person; and that you wanta be like him. I had this joker bringing me candy, magazines, cigars and he mailed a couple of birthday cards for me. I always told him he shouldn't do things like that 'cause he could get in trouble and then I would hint around for something else I needed. Pretty soon he'd bring it, but I made him feel I was looking out for his welfare. Then I figured it was about time I got a little more serious with this guy.

One day a fight broke out in the wing and my duck tried to stop it. He wound up facing a couple of cons with knives who said they hated cops and were going to kill him. He was scared spitless. I let him stay in that situation for a while then finally rushed in, got between the cop and the cons and talked them out of hurting him. I never saw a guy so grateful. Right at that time this duck said he'd do just about anything for me. I told him friends needed to stick together; that no one should expect favors for doing what was right. That night, I used Pete's own cigarettes to pay off the guys who staged the fight for me.

Sometime later I showed this officer a letter from my sister stating the wife of a guy in our wing had been killed in an accident. The con was a friend of mine so I asked my duck to tell the guy. He couldn't do it because he gets too emotional he said, so I wound up telling the inmate myself.

When you're grooming a duck you are limited only by your own imagination. Here are two situations that I set-up to learn something about the dude. The fight told me fear and friendship could get me what I wanted from this cop, and the second added sympathy to the list.

Everyone in the wing was sad over the loss of this convict's wife, especially the cop, so the next day I brought my duck a sympathy card signed by most of the cons in the unit and told him they had taken up a collection for the con's kids. I told him I knew it was against the rules, and that convicts ain't supposed to have money, but this was different. This would do a lot of good. "There ought to be some rules we can break," I said. "Most of us convicts have spent a lifetime taking things from people, and the one time we want to give, there's a rule against it. It just doesn't seem right!" The cop was concerned over the amount of money with the card and that he might get caught. At about this point my personality began changing a little. I had to let this guy know he had already done some dumb things that could get him into trouble—to do so in a way that showed we were still good friends but that I meant business. So I reminded him of a few past situations. For the first time, he didn't quite know how to take me. I immediately got nice again. I said, "Ah, come on, it would do us a lot of good to give for once in our lives, you can't deny a person that kind of inner satisfaction. Any doctor will tell you it's good therapy. Besides, the penalty for taking a letter out with money in it ain't no greater than the penalty for the ones you've already taken out. Don't get me wrong, I would never tell, but I have had some trouble keeping some of these other cats in the unit from telling the sergeant that's always on your back." He was beginning to feel the pressure. The confusion in his face was obvious. He wasn't sure where I stood. As I continued talking, I slid the envelope into his inside jacket pocket. "There ain't no way you'll be caught. They don't search cops like they do inmates. Gosh, man, you can't let little kids starve just 'cause their old man is in the joint. Those kids ain't done no wrong. There ain't a cop in this place who would understand the deep hurt a person goes through when someone they love gets killed. I thought you were different. You don't have to worry, we took care of those people who might have snitched to the sarg. No way are we going to let you get in trouble. Besides, I'll never ask for a favor like this again. It's just that those kids . . . " I walked away and left him to think about what I had just said.

I had been my old friendly self for a few days so my duck could become comfortable over taking the letter and money out. Then I told him some relatives of my inmate friend—the deceased woman's husband—would be sending a package to his house. The package would contain nothing but prayer beads for the grieving inmate. "Don't open the box 'til you get here," I told him. "We need the address to thank these people, and they were really grateful to get that money." He agreed. When the package came, I told the cop I'd show him the contents later and he said never mind he didn't want to know. His voice told me I needed to butter him up a little because we both knew he was over a barrel. I had him right where I wanted him. But I still had to develop him more— deeper. I knew he was in debt on the streets so I got the train- ing officer's clerk (an inmate) to add extra time on the dude's pay records. The cop appreciated the extra money and he said nothing. Because I let him know I was responsible for this little favor, he became more friendly, but he was still cautious with me. By this time I was about the only friend this cop had. Sometime back his real friends began telling the guy he was being too friendly with convicts. I couldn't let that go on, so I started a rumor that this cat was living with an inmate's wife. He came under investigation. Cops like to go with winners, not losers. This guy was a loser so they left him alone. He had to talk to someone, and I was the only person available. I had the guy right where I wanted him, for sure! It took time but you gotta develop a duck carefully if you want it to pay off. Now the guy was ready for the big one. He had to do anything I said or I tossed him to the wolves.

84

Turning the Duck into a Golden Goose

I had done a lot of time in my life and was tired of prison. I wanted to get out. I'd been thinking about this for a long time now. Getting out had become an obsession with me. My duck and I were about the same size so I got him off to the side and said, "You don't know it yet, but I'm going on parole, and you're going to help me get there!" My voice was stern and commanding. He looked confused, but he knew I meant business.

"I want you to bring me in a cop's uniform!" We had joked about this kind of thing before and he hoped I was still kidding. With all the hatred I could muster I shouted, "Look, you stupid S.O.B., you ain't got no choice! Every convict in this wing will snitch you off. You took out letters, money, you brought in things we still have stored to use as evidence against you, and you've been accepting money from the state under false pretenses. Now you bring in that damn uniform or you're dead, sucker!" I stood glaring at him and let what I had just said sink in for a moment. Then I handed him a letter from the people who had received the money in the letter he had taken out. It stated they were willing to testify against him. He had no choice. He had to do as I told him. "Listen, you rotten bastard," I continued, "you bring a shirt tomorrow, trousers the next day and so on until I have the complete uniform. DO YOU UNDERSTAND?!"

The duck brought a piece of the uniform each day in his lunch box. As I received them I rolled each new item and neatly placed it in the bottom of my foot locker. Then I told this dumb cop to call me off my job whenever the institution search team came into the wing. "Make some excuse like I didn't clean my room," I told him. I knew if I were on hand when my room was being searched, I could talk the searcher out of going too far into my locker.

85

Some cops do their job and look at everything in the room, but most of them don't like searching and can easily be talked out of looking in places where a lot of work is involved. You know, there's a psychology behind handling a searcher. One of the first things convicts learn when they come to a joint is how to beat the search team. Like, if you want to hide a major contraband item in your room, then you leave a minor contraband item so it can be discovered. The dude searching will usually abandon the search when he finds the piece you salted, and he leaves feeling he's done a fine job. You got to be just a little bit smarter than they are to survive in prison. On the other hand, there is that occasional sharp cop who can't be fooled. When this happens, you're in trouble. So the way you handle this guy is you get all the cons in the area to complain about how the guy dumps stuff on your floor, tears your bedding, etc. If the complaints keep coming about the guy, joint big shots take the attitude that "where there's smoke there must be fire," and they give him a job change. Can you beat that? The dude gets punished because he's doing a better job than anyone else.

One morning my duck called and said the search team was going to be in his unit. I rushed inside and stood nonchalantly by my cell door. A cop was already in my room searching. I was polite, joked with him, pointed to an area in my room he failed to search. I even complimented him on his thoroughness. When he came to the foot locker I said, "Man, I'm sorry, it's going to take you hours to get through all the junk in that box." By seeding this thought he gets tired just looking at the job. They'll usually just give the box a once over lightly and quit. I pointed to a master list of things in the foot locker that was taped to the underside of the lid. I said that because the box was so full the list might make the job more bearable; that it was packed military style; and it took me hours to do it. "But you got your job to do," I emphasized, "and I don't mind repacking, even though it will take me most of the day—go ahead on." The dude was impressed by my politeness and complimentary attitude and he was convincing himself that a con who encourages a thorough search is probably clean. I did ask him, however, that as he took things out of the locker to place them on the bed—if he didn't mind; and that he could glance at the list to see how orderly I kept my things.

By saying this, I knew two things would take place in his mind: his eyes would check the list as I suggested; when he consistently found things in order, he'd feel he's wasting his time; and the old army buddy association I was developing would help convince him I was hiding nothing. So I figured after removing a few things he would conclude the search.

It happened just as I thought. He removed the top row of clothing and about half of the next, then said, "O.K., you're clear," and he moved on to the next cell.

"Whew." Breathing a sigh of relief, I decided this searcher came a little too close and I had better put my escape plan in action soon. Tomorrow morning, I thought, was as good a time as any.

My duck comes on duty at 7:45 a.m. At 8:00 a.m. the night shift goes home, and at the same time there is a major work release for prisoners: the corridor is always crowded at that time. I figured I had 15 minutes to get out of my room, slip into the broom closet, get into the uniform, then melt into the crowd unnoticed. I would go to the exit door next to the control room where a sergeant is supposed to identify everyone leaving and stand with the group of officers waiting to go home. The procedure for releasing officers from the security area at this joint is done like this: The sergeant at the control room looks at everyone wanting into the sallyport (a sallyport is a holding area in between two locked steel doors). When he's satisfied he's only releasing staff, he pushes a button which opens the first of two electronically controlled doors. Everyone enters and the first door closes. Before the second door is opened, an officer looks at everyone to assure the sergeant made no mistakes. Once the second door is opened they cross a patio to the administration building where another sallyport exists, and the procedure is repeated. When everyone passes through the administration building, there is a final sallyport where a tower man and a sergeant make sure the proper people enter and leave. In each of those sallyports, the employees who opened the doors were nightshift people and I had suspected that because they were tired and sleepy, they released people not on the basis of positive identification, but because they wore a uniform. Well, at any rate, tomorrow morning I would find out how correct my suspicions were.

The night passed slowly. I had a difficult time sleeping, so I spent most of the night going over and over every detail of the escape plan. Finally it was 7:45 a.m. I heard the lock on my door snap, and I knew it was my duck letting me out. I grabbed the uniform and rushed to the broom closet. The uniform fit like a glove! It's funny how clothes can make you feel. I suddenly felt clean, almost like I wished I were on the side of the law and not a criminal. Then I thought of my stupid duck and decided I was better off as a hood.

During morning work release, the day shift officers stand in the center of the corridor as inmates pass up and down the long hallway on their way to job assignments. Staff members going home walk along one wall to the control room and they usually are looking into the units being released; their faces are away from the officers in the corridor, so it would not be suspicious if I did the same. I started out of the unit. As I passed the officers' stations, I took my duck's lunch box for realism. He started to object and I said, "Don't say it, you dummy, or you're dead." I slipped into the crowd and made my way to control. The sergeant was peering through the mirror identifying people. Then suddenly the bolt snapped and the electric door opened. Everyone stepped into the sallyport, and the door closed behind us. I kept my head down slightly so no one could get a direct look at my face. The officer looked everyone over from a small unbreakable window, and he was being careful. I thought it might be over at this point. The officer's phone rang, some people were turning in and drawing keys, and in his momentary distraction, he opened the second door.

When I was crossing the patio to the administration building, an officer coming on duty stopped me and asked me for a match. I felt panic surge through my veins. If the group got through the first door without me I would be alone, and alone, an unfamiliar officer was certain to be challenged. I searched my pockets quickly and said, "Sorry, guess I'm out of matches, too." I hurried and caught the group just as the first door opened. The desk officer was flirting with a little blond secretary and just let everyone pass because they were all uniform personnel. The last sallyport was about 75 feet in front of us and the hardest one to get through. An officer in the tower by the entrance building—main gate as it was called—would identify the people leaving. If he recognized everyone, he would open the first gate. Once we're inside the sallyport, the main gate sergeant checks everyone a final time before the gate to freedom can be opened.

As the group approached this final sallyport my heart was in my throat. I began to think for the first time there was a possibility of my making it, even though I knew this would be my hardest hurdle. Everyone had now reached the gate. I kept my head low without being obvious about it. The tower man was scanning faces. Then he shouted, "You there, look up!" I didn't know if he was talking to me but assumed he was. I shadowed my face with my hand like I was trying to keep the sun from blinding me and looked up, slightly waving my hand at him to indicate I recognized him. A long moment passed, then the door slid open. While waiting for the final check, I noticed a large group of officers standing in the main gate sergeants' station ready to be admitted after the night crew were identified and released. I heard someone in our group say they were new officers going on an orientation tour. The gate sergeant's eyes were scanning the group. I was trying to be inconspicuous by looking slightly away from him. It seemed an eternity of silence was being lived in those few moments. Then, my world fell apart when he shouted, "You, the officer with his back to me, come over here." I approached the window he was looking through and this time I looked him right in the eye. I felt disappointed and angry over being so close and getting caught, and I had about decided to suddenly hit the fence even though I knew the tower man would shoot at me. I was mad enough to take that chance. The sergeant asked, "What are you doing in there? You're supposed to be with these new officers out here."

Thinking quickly, I replied in an apologetic voice, "I'm sorry, sarg. But I thought the training officer said to meet him in the administration building."

"Who the hell let you in anyway?" The sergeant sorta growled in a tone indicating he was irritated with me. He opened the gate, and as I entered the gate house, he stood in front of me and demanded, "Now you stay with your group, understand?"

"Yes—I will—sir. But do I have time to run to my car before the training officer gets here? I forgot my I.D. card."

The sergeant looked disgusted. "There's one in every group. All right, make it fast, the lieutenant doesn't like to be kept waiting!"

I hurried to the far end of the main parking lot. Behind the last row of cars was a fence separating a corn field. I dropped to my knees behind a car and crawled on my stomach and slid under the barbed wire fence to the safety of the tall corn stalks. Keeping low I made my way to the main highway. I saw a car parked on the highway shoulder. No one was in it, so I assumed the driver had run out of gas. I decided to stand in front of the car and hitchhike. My thinking was that being in uniform and in front of the parked car, drivers would think it was mine and I had experienced car troubles. It worked! I had been standing about two minutes when this car pulled over. The driver motioned me to hurry when I noticed he was wearing the same kind of uniform I had on; my heart dropped. What was worse I recognized him as one of the wing officers at the joint I just left. I was caught. "Get in," he said sharply. I almost confessed "O.K., you caught me, I'll go peacefully," but I didn't. The lump in my throat wouldn't let me.

"Where to?" he asked with a half smile.

"The first town you come to so I can get some gas," I managed to answer. The town was about 20 miles away. As we drove, I gathered my wits. He said he'd help me get the gas and run me back to the car. He asked if I was a new employee at the joint and I was glad to confess I was. Then I said, "You don't need to return me to the car. I'll call my wife and she'll pick me up."

"O.K.," he said, "it's no bother—you know, you sure remind me of someone I've met before!"

"Really? Well . . . no! I'm sure we've never met," I said.

He dropped me at a service station, wished me well, and drove away. I was FREE!

About three days later, I was miles away from the prison. I was hungry and tired so I decided to rob a store near the outskirts of the nearby city. During that robbery, I killed three people, but managed to keep from getting caught for over a year. Never mind how I got the gun. I was eventually apprehended, convicted and returned. I hated that stupid cop I ducked, and while I was on the streets my obsession to get a message to authorities so that cat would be fired was the thing which led to my apprehension and new conviction. Eventually I had to testify at his trial. Of course I couldn't tell them much except that I had developed the duck and then all the details of the cop's violations. "Anything else you folks would like to know?" I asked my interviewers.

"Only one thing. Now that you are back in prison, are you trying to acquire, or have you acquired another duck?"

I leaned back in my chair, fixed my eyes on the petitioner as I thought about the question, took a stick of chewing gum from my shirt pocket, unwrapped it, and slowly slid it into my mouth. I stood to leave the room, paused at the door, smiled, and said, "They don't sell gum in these joints . . . later, man!"

Legal Apprehension of Manipulators

This section is necessarily short because legal apprehension of a set-up team or individual is extremely difficult. Hard evidence cannot be obtained during any of the set-up steps until the program calls for the inclusion of a shopping list, a lever, or the sting because only these last three steps cannot be introduced without an obvious violation of institution rules or breaking the law. Evidence obtained prior to this is largely circumstantial or based on suspicion, and herein lies the barrier.

Supervisors will not usually give the case the credence it deserves, and any attempts to interrogate the involved prisoners only produce temporary compliant behavior. Interrogators become impatient in these situations because evidence is only suspect, and they attempt to get at the truth through prolonged or repetitive interviewing. In doing so, the interrogator incurs the risk of uncooperative behavior without eliciting any information to substantiate the accuser's suspicions. The most complete and accurate information that can hope to be obtained using the interview tactics can be only further suspicion.

Use of the polygraph in these situations can be helpful, but only to aid in substantiating the employee's accusations. The success rate even then can only be estimated at the rate of 50 percent. The polygraph is based upon physiological responses and considers such things as changes in systolic blood pressure, galvanic skin resonses, pulse rate, muscular tension, etc. The unimpressive 50 percent success rate causes concern in placing proof of guilt because of the variables or "spinover" that can affect polygraph testing such as relationship of operator and subject; prior indoctrination of subject; the ability of the person being questioned to control psychological and physiological functions; and the interrogator's interpretation of data. These all have an effect on the rate of deception that can be detected. Even if a person "fails" the lie detector and it is obvious that the inmate is guilty of fraudulent manipulation, this evidence cannot be used to initiate or substantiate any disciplinary action. Unless there is an actual rules violation, it is extremely difficult to point an accusing finger and have it stick.

What then can people do who suspect they have been selected as the victim of a compromise? There are several things that can be done to assure the employee of protection without fear of criticism, and any one or combination of the protectors listed in the following section will have the effect of drawing the set-up process to a swift conclusion. It is the responsibility of the employee, however, to decide which protector is applicable to his or her situation.

Protectors

~~~~~~

Important traits for prisoner rehabilitation include self-satisfaction and a sense of accomplishment. The personal gain achieved by coercement seems self-satisfying to the manipulator, but only for the moment. The deception causes as the end result a feeling of self-defeat.

Employees set the stage for manipulation by deluding themselves about the methods inmates want for control. Some believe approaching inmates on a convict level, such as using profanity and inmate jargon, obtains the best results. But these employees dive to the inmate level of interaction and fail to raise the inmate up to higher standards and values. They miss the point of the earlier defined professionalism and retard the rehabilitation process. Prisoners want good examples to emulate. They want employees to prove that a life style based on honesty and other good values surpasses a life style based on crime.

Other employees, and the majority of past staff members who were dismissed, felt or reacted as if only kindness and understanding controlled inmate actions most effectively. Of course inmates encouraged this self-serving idea by praising this kindness and then expressing to the employee that command tones were inconsistent with the past pleasing personality. For the sake of maintaining the "nice guy" image, victims fell into a pattern of behavior leading to inconsistent rule enforcement and the inability to say NO. Kindness and concern as effective control tools work well, but not at the expense of losing control.

Correctional employees have an obligation to prevent crime—not contribute to it, and any act aiding manipulation sinks the prisoner into greater depths of depression. So in order to help employees professionally progress and help inmates rehabilitate, a list of protectors are included.

Protector Number One: understand the definition of a professional and strive to act like one.

Protector Number Two: learn to recognize the steps to a set-up and take proper action. "Nip it in the bud," so to speak.

Protector Number Three: understand that communication consists of a sender and a receiver. New employees must very quickly learn that messages sent or received by people in confinement differ markedly from those sent or received by people in the free society. Employees must constantly monitor the seemingly casual inmate remarks as well as their own responses. For a more detailed explanation, read Responses and Reasoning that follows this section.

Protector Number Four: learn to say NO and mean it. Saying NO to a person the employee has befriended or tried to help always remains a difficult task. Interestingly, two of the smallest words in the English vocabulary—*yes* and *no*— are the hardest to use, and in the prison setting, any staff member probably uses *no* more than *yes*. There are actually three types of *no:* there is the *no* that says to the inmate, "If you keep at me I'll probably do it"; there is the *no* that says, "Today it's no, tomorrow I may feel differently"; and then there is the *no* that says just that—NO! The command NO can be administered politely, but with firm stand and conviction without generating animosity. Inmates appreciate knowing where they stand, and where the employee will draw the line.

The information chrono (see Protector Number Nine) is an excellent tool for an employee who has not as yet mastered the command NO (this has been known to especially apply to some non-custody women whose job assignment involves supervising or interacting with inmates). Some people can say no, no no, and inmates, interpret it as no, but never NO. Somehow the message included a hint of hesitancy, or unsurety, even though the sender really wanted to say NO. Inmates are persistent, so an employee has to select the most effective protector, either verbal or written, that applies to each situation.

Protector Number Five: be in command of your area.

For new employees, this sometimes poses a difficult problem because they may not be sure of procedures, details, or how to command. Manipulators easily spot new employees and are more than happy to "fill them in" on details. This, they hope, will establish an over-familiar relationship at the onset, which of course can lead to getting special favors and cashing in on the employee's feelings of obligation. It is essential that new staff members seek information about the prison community from staff as quickly as possible for their own safety, or to save themselves future embarrassment as the victims of a set-up.

Some new employees may have another kind of problem regarding command. Throughout the United States, most

97

prisons and jail facilities require their custodial personnel to wear uniforms—a sign of authority. Uniforms can be a valuable aid for control and a deterrent from trouble. But a uniform, in and of itself, cannot command or control: that function belongs to the person the apparel adorns. Most prison custodial personnel perform effectively with or without this authoritarian symbol, but some desperately need its help. It symbolizes their authority, their protection, their strength and their power. Without it they flounder. They hide behind the uniform. Also, some custodial officers have the mistaken idea that when on duty they control, but when performing prison program functions after hours, they have no authority. A street wise prisoner soon discovers which officers need an authority symbol and which ones do not. Consider the following.

Rose, a correctional officer, desperately wanted to keep her job, but her supervisors felt she was incapable of controlling inmates. She had been observed overlooking minor rules violations. She enforced rules for some inmates and not for others. She was easily distracted. She felt obligated to inmates who were nice to her and gave them special privileges. She was far too friendly with a select group of inmates, and she could not work in harmony with her fellow officers. The captain had informed her that come the end of the month she would have to seek employment elsewhere.

Rose had been a correctional officer less than a year and during that time inmates observed her, tested her, supported, protected, and empathized with her. They turned staff against her, and she against them, and now they had discovered something in her past she had been trying to conceal from her supervisors and peers—her sister was addicted to drugs and she herself had used them. After duty hours Rose supervised a prison self-help group. She was not a person who could control, but inmates noticed that when she wore her uniform she was a great deal more aggressive than when she did not, so they asked her to wear "street" clothes in group sessions. When she did not comply, they demanded she not wear her official garments because of the inhibiting effect on the group. Without the uniform, Rose had no control at all; she was stripped of all authority.

It was at this point that correctional trainers helped Rose realize she had become the victim of a set-up. They showed her the *pattern* of a set-up. She recognized that all of the seemingly unrelated incidents were actually tied tightly together. She realized that her interactions with the inmates fit precisely into the set-up pattern. Then the trainers taught her how to stop the process, retake command, and how to control her area. They pointed out that she was a correctional officer on or off duty, in or out of uniform, twenty-four hours a day. In the days that followed, Rose became such an effective officer, the institution extended her probationary period and now considers her one of their better employees.

Rose made a mistake that is not uncommon in corrections. She felt command, control and treatment entailed separate entities, each requiring a different personality approach. To her, custody and treatment were opposites that could never be aligned. As an eight hour a day cop, she sometimes managed to practice the hardness that she felt a uniform required, but she was inconsistent in its application. As a treatment program supervisor, she became excessively soft, because what little authority she could call upon was hanging at home in her closet.

When she discovered that control and treatment were essential to each other; that she could maintain a pleasant, consistent personality while setting aside nonsense; and learned to apply the unfamiliar friendship concept, inmates and staff alike recognized her ability to take charge, and effectively perform her job and her supervisory duties. She became pleased with her newly found approach; became more confident; gained respect from both staff and inmates; and realized that she could be a cop twenty-four hours a day. She no longer had to hide behind her uniform.

All employees attempting to maintain control of their area should make sure they are firm, fair and consistent. One officer, while setting aside nonsense, but not being aware of prisoners who try to do good and not manipulate, sternly asked an inmate, "What are you doing in my area?"

The reply was an eye-opener. "I've lived here for eight months. You only notice the trouble-makers. You give them the best jobs just to keep them in line. What do you suggest I do to get one of the better jobs?" The officer still maintained control but changed his criteria for job holders.

Inmates notice when an employee gains control. Said of one secretary who had recently completed a course on assertiveness training, "She used to be fun to play on until she took that darn course. We can't even make her feel obligated for our favors anymore." They respect control, but still try to finagle a way to take it back.

One device inmates who are leaving a job assignment use to usurp control is to strongly recommend another inmate for the job. The reason could come from two distinct possibilities. (1) The inmate could boast that he has an "in" with the employee and that the job is his to sell. This gives him status as well as payment. Or (2) A turner may feel that he is not making enough progress in the set-up and sees a need to replace himself with another member of the team. In either case, the employee has relinquished control and some respect.

Inmates appreciate employees who take command and who consult staff, not inmates, for their information. If an inmate truly needs help, he will consult employees whom he respects for their fairness, consistency and strength—not employees he condescendingly views as gullible.

Protector Number Six: check the central file of inmates whom the employee feels is trying to get "too close" or who work for the employee. In a prison, it is important to know the kind of convict the employee is dealing with when offering special or day-to-day help or guidance. Some employees voice the opinion that each inmate can come to them with a clean slate. This may sound good on the surface but "knowledge is power": in a prison, employees need this power to truly help the real problems of an inmate and to cut off any deceit the inmate may be implicated in. When the inmate realizes he cannot get away with "duping the guy," he will respect the employee and (after a testing period) not try to pull any more shenanigans.

The employees should realize that much of the information given by inmates can be verified or nullified in their central files. Inmates know this and (contacts) observe the employee's frequency of doing so. If supplied information is verified by the central file or other staff members, then the employee should ask himself, "Is this requested help part of my job description or is it a request 'friend to friend'?" If the requested help comes within the employee's realm, then help as designated should be offered to the fullest extent. If it does not, a person who has that job description and is perhaps more qualified should be recommended. If the employee should decided to accept the request, it should be done cautiously (make sure none of the set-up steps are involved), openly (make sure the inmate knows you cleared it with someone), and in a friendly, business-like manner (be professional).

Protector Number Seven: be knowledgeable of proper institutional procedures relating to avenues inmates can pursue to acquire needs not covered in the institution rule book. Inmates can usually get anything reasonable they need. For example, one inmate clerk asked the secretary for whom he worked if she would make a photostatic copy of his legal document because he wanted to send the good news to his parents. She knew that this was a case-worker's job, but also knew that they were very busy. Since she did not know the proper procedure, she referred the inmate to her supervisor.

After the inmate submitted a trust withdrawal for ten cents, the secretary was free to make the copy for him. The employee was seen by the supervisor as helpful, but only openly and through the proper channels. The employee was seen by the inmate as helpful, but not someone who will allow a you/me situation. A ten cent lever is a powerful tool.

Protector Number Eight: the intended victim must let someone know he or she is being cultivated, and let the inmate responsible know the incidents are out in the open. Why is it important to tell someone and to let the inmate know of the exposure? Simply this: Any street psychologist knows that a secret between two people gives one or the other the advantage of taking liberties if the secret is to be kept. To illustrate, assume an inmate implied Ms. Jordon might take out a letter. She refuses and elects to keep the incident to herself. The inmate contrues her unwillingness to take action as a weakness and as silent approval. If no action is taken he will continue the pressure. On the other hand, she might think, "If I tell my supervisor or a fellow employee every time an inmate asks me to do something a little off color I'm going to appear paranoid. I'll be running to them all the time and they may feel I'm unable to do the job." This feeling has validity and truth to it. Yet no action at all means the requests will continue. "So," she asks, "how can it be done?"

If Ms. Jordon feels the incident is too minor to report and that her peers might feel she is overly suspicious, but she still has that "gut level" feeling of being tested, then she should talk it out with a fellow employee or the inmate's supervisor in front of the inmate. For example, suppose an inmate volunteers to mop and wax her office. He is not assigned to Ms. Jordon as an orderly, so she would be accepting a favor from him. She is a little uneasy because she fears he may want a favor in return, yet she does not want to imply the gesture is dishonest if it is not. Telling her supervisor that she suspects a set-up may cause him to respond by saying, "What are you, paranoid? That sort of thing is done all the time!" The solution, then, is simply to explain to the inmate that she appreciates his offer and the two of them will talk it over with his supervisor to assure she is not infringing on his time. This keeps the actions and agreements out in the open and eliminates any you/me situation.

The importance of telling someone in front of the inmate or letting the inmate know you shared, cannot be stressed enough. The set-up practitioner does not want anyone to know or even suspect devious actions for fear of detection. When he knows a staff member keeps everything in the open, the set-up process is usually concluded.

Those who have used protector number eight have unknowingly been fortunate in that they noticed a change in inmate behavior but did not know why. These employees now attribute the change to the act of consulting staff on matters instead of relying on inmate advice. The inmates knew these staff exposed all interactions conducted with their wards.

Employees not in custody positions may feel that inmates are getting too friendly but do not know how to handle the situation or have not acquired the command NO. In these cases, the employees should consult the custody staff, and after giving the inmate's name, ask them to speak with him. The inmate will definitely know that it is out in the open and that custody is watching. Detection is not wanted by inmates.

Protector Number Nine: write an information chrono (a brief report that is placed in an inmate's central file in the record's office) and make sure the original goes in the central file with copies going to the writer, the supervisor and the inmate. The writer is not requesting any administrative action—only exposure. Inmates do not care to have illicit actions recorded because when a pattern of their behavior develops in their file, it can affect their future, i.e., one recorded suspicion will not really harm the inmate, but several by different authors can. Staff members researching the inmate's file are alerted to the inmate's capabilities, and now the responsible party has an extremely difficult time setting someone else up. Also this pattern of behavior alerts hearing representatives and they can assume rehabilitation is not occurring.

Recorded information has the effect of stopping a set-up immediately, at least by that particular inmate. A sample information chrono could read as follows:

Inmate Doaks, B-0026, has recently requested a series of small favors and has been inquiring into my personal life. Although he has not violated any rules or policy, his requests seem headed in that direction. To date he has jokingly hinted at my giving him cigarettes, gum, pencils, and he has asked about my financial affairs. I neither appreciate nor desire this attention, and if it does not cease, I will take stronger action.

The inmate (usually a runner or hopeful turner) whose name appears on the chrono will visit the writer only one more time. His farewell consists of (1) asking why it was written because (2) it is certainly not what he intended you to think,—you are wrong about him, (3) a statement that he is sorry you feel that way and (4) perhaps a request that you retract the chrono. In the cases that were studied, this particular inmate was never seen again by the employee who wrote the chrono.

104

Protector Number Ten: write a behavior chrono. In the set-up testing process, inmates violate minor rules to find an employee's tolerance level. These violations may not be serious enough for strong disciplinary action, but they may be too serious for an informational chrono. In that case the staff member would want to use a behavioral chrono. A sample of how this tool can be used is as follows:

Inmate Smith, B-3974, comes to my office on a daily basis requesting favors such as . . . . He is not assigned to this area and I have told him on several occasions not to come here. He refuses to heed my warnings so on this date I gave him a direct order. Failure to comply this time will result in a disciplinary report.

Protector Number Eleven: write a disciplinary report. This form is used when the inmate request or action is an obvious violation of the rules. It is an excellent exposure tool and can be designed to fit any violation whether administrative or serious. An example of this report is as follows:

On March 1, 1980, at approximately 11:00 a.m., Inmate John Doe B-0006 requested that I bring in a bottle of wine by smuggling it through the main gate of the institution in my lunch box and presenting it to him when I assume my post in D-Unit. He stated that my failure to comply would result in a statement from him and other inmates attesting to the fact that I have already smuggled in cookies and candy. He said he has the evidence in his cell and exposure would result in the loss of my job. It is true that I made an error in judgment and on occasions shared items from my lunch box that I did not care to eat. I am willing to accept whatever disciplinary action is entailed as a result of my mistake, but that does not alter the fact that Inmate Doe is in violation of institution rule 3008, and I am hereby citing him for that violation.

105

This is an actual report and it makes one very important point: Not all violations of rules, or mistakes in judgment result in criticism or employment termination of the employee. In this case, as in one mentioned earlier, the hearing officer complimented the staff member for admitting his mistake and stated the incident would make him a much better employee. On disciplinary reports, the employee should expect some inmate backlash which is discussed later in the text.

Protector Number Twelve: one of the most important, if not THE most important, concerns knowing what to do in a crisis situation. When prisoners present their shopping list (demand for illegal contraband) it will *always* be when the staff member is alone. The request may be made on a one to one basis, but the manipulator might also have his buddies with him. The demand is illegal. Prisoners know this and they also know they are in trouble if the staff member refuses. This is a dangerous situation because they may decide to use force.

It is best for the employee to remain noncommittal by saying something like, "I need time to think it over, or time to get the stuff." Once free of the individual or group, the victim should go immediately and report them. The employee should admit to any mistakes he or she may have made. Far better for the victim to face criticism, suspension or even dismissal than to become deeply involved in crime. Direct face-to-face refusal with statements like, "I'll report you, I'll have you locked up," etc., are not only foolish, but they force manipulators into using stronger measures.

If the victim is a woman who has just been asked for sex, she can request time to think it over. This should work because the team feels she really may succumb to their wishes and will wait a bit longer to reap such rewards. If the inmates will wait for her reply, she should report the incident immediately and issue a direct order in writing that the involved inmates are prohibited in her area of work. If it does not work, she can scream to attract attention. If that fails she can faint.

Using Protectors

The next two cases are almost identical except the institutions and the contraband items sought by prisoners differed; one officer permitted the crime, the other prevented the crime; one officer was ignorant of protectors, the other was not.

Wanting to show inmates his appreciation for their hard work, an officer brought cookies from his home to reward them. He knew the institution permitted the practice, but only with prior administrative permission. He had gotten permission before, but he reasoned that the boss always did it and no one but the inmates would know anyway. Cookies were no big thing; acquiring permission would take too long, he had the cookies, and the reward was due now. He was doing something nice and what possible harm could come from rewarding inmates for a good job with a few cookies?

The day following the distribution of the gift, prisoners in the officer's work crew told him to pick up hamburgers for the crew from the employee snack bar. Arrangements had been made with the inmate cook to have them ready at no cost. When the officer refused, prisoners promptly threatened to report the cookie incident to his supervisor. The officer, not wanting to be criticized, complied with the demand. As this practice continued, prison administrators somehow became aware the officer was not paying for food supplied to his work crew, and the situation culminated in embarrassment for the staff member and punishment for the prisoners.

Inmates on his work crew had been working hard and praising him as a testing process without him realizing it. They suspected he was susceptible to manipulation and created a situation making it difficult to refuse. During disciplinary proceedings, the inmates verbalized their disdain for the staff member stating he was a "duck."

Had the officer been properly trained, this incident would never have taken place. Conditions leading to the man's embarrassment, the workcrew's punishment, and the adverse staff/inmate relations are enumerated.

* He failed to follow procedure and acquire permission reward good behavior with the cookies. Inmates were aware he was breaking the rules.
* He, himself, acted dishonestly by not paying for the sandwiches.
* He provided prisoners with a lever for manipulation.
* By circumventing minor rules, he lost inmate respect.
* His failure to report the hamburger incident caused loss of command and control. This led to embarrassment for himself and punishment for the prisoners.
* His actions retarded the inmate treatment process.

In the second case, the officer in charge of a workcrew became suspicious when the prisoners under his supervision began producing at a rate inconsistent with their normal pattern. He accepted their compliments politely and, in the hope of inducing continuance of the behavior, acquired permission to reward his crew effort with sweet rolls from the snack bar which he purchased with his own funds. When issuing the reward, he mentioned permission to do so had been approved.

Several days later, members of the officer's workcrew asked the man to bring in cigarettes, stating other supervisors do it all the time without bothering to acquire permission. Before responding to the request, the officer signaled to one of his peers for assistance in the event his refusal to comply caused inmates to become unruly. While rejecting the request, his attitude was polite but firm and bore the admonishment of disciplinary action if such requests were repeated in the future. Otherwise, the matter would be recorded on a general information report and forgotten. Via the inmate grapevine, word went out to other prisoners that inmates were safe working for this man. "He took care of business, but was fair," they said. His area would not be a trouble spot for prisoners.

Both staff and inmates felt this officer's application of justice addressed the situation fairly, which resulted in a waiting list of prisoners who wanted to work for him. Unlike the officer involved in the cookie incident, this staff member—using the concept of observation, recognition, prevention—proceeded in the following manner.

* He knew the usual pattern of inmate work production and noticed this crew produced at a higher rate. (P.N. 1, 5)
* He rewarded their efforts and let his workcrew know permission to do so had been obtained. (P.N. 7, 8)
* He followed procedure and gave inmates no reason to believe he would circumvent the rules. (P.N. 3, 7)
* Prisoners could not demand cigarettes—only ask—because they had no lever to use against the officer. (P.N. 3, 8)
* Even when asked for contraband, his actions prevented his own victimization and prevented inmate punishment. (P.N. 1, 2, 4)
* During the incident, he continued to keep everything in the open, and by calling for peer aid, his actions were witnessed in addition to having help available in case the situation got out of hand. (P. N. 8, 12)
* He took immediate action so no one suffered embarrassment—the set-up was prevented before it got started. (P.N. 2, 4, 12)
* He did or said nothing he would be ashamed to share with his fellow employees, and he reported the incident. (P.N. 1, 3, 8, 9)
* He retained control and command of his area and crew and displayed actions which generated respect. (P.N. 1, 5)

109

* Morale improved markedly for the officer and his work crew. (P.N. 1)
* Because of his actions, work production continued to increase. Staff/inmate relations were improved, and prisoners felt safe working for him. (P.N. 1, 3, 5)
* He had taken the trouble to obtain training in set-up techniques which provided him with an awareness the other staff member in the first case did not possess. (P.N. 2)
* He improved the professional image of correctional officers, set an excellent example, established a good reputation, improved his own confidence and self-image, and maintained personal dignity and integrity for himself and the people he supervised. (P.N. 1, 3, 5, 7)

A
Questionnaire
with
Answers

The following is a list of actual statements or situations used by inmates testing prison or jail employees in their effort to determine which staff members would be susceptible to manipulation. Inmates know that law enforcement places heavy emphasis on the practice of professionalism, and that most employees strive to develop its principles. Open and obvious attacks on a person's professional values would be met with strong resistance, so inmates design their actions and verbal presentations to subtly shave the edge of professionalism. To illustrate, two officers observe one inmate strike another for no apparent reason. One observer concludes the assailant acted wrongly and should be punished. The other elects to withhold judgment until all facts surrounding the altercation are gathered and understood. Both staff members consider themselves professional, but without realizing it, the one pronouncing immediate judgment has sliced the edge of

111

his professional approach. This person conveys a clear message: under given circumstances his or her judgment and reasoning supersedes professional training. Any inmate manipulator observing the interchange may decide to apply additional pressures to determine other areas in which the officer would once again set aside professional practices.

When responding to the information that follows, the reader should refer to the concept of the familiar and unfamiliar friends discussed in the DEFINITION AND TERMS section of this book. In making decisions, keep in mind that professionals are unfamiliar friends, and that even unfamiliar friends have the responsibility of taking command to prevent a friend from acting inappropriately. Helping a friend may require commands or orders that are direct and harsh, but the risk is taken without hesitation when help is needed. Using this frame of reference, decide upon an appropriate response to each of the following situations, and determine whether or not the message sent (in the prison setting) asks to be a candidate for manipulation. In most of the samples mentioned on the next few pages, employees that were being tested responded in a manner impressing inmates of their vulnerability. Some were selected as victims of a set-up, and were eventually either embarrassed, suffered termination of employment for illegal acts, or were injured by inmates for refusing their demands.

A QUESTIONNAIRE

What would you do if . . .

1. An inmate of the opposite sex said, "I think you're beautiful?"
2. An inmate of the opposite sex says, "I want your body?"
3. You have just placed an order in the employee snackbar and the inmate orderly whispers, "No charge for officers who treat prisoners as nice as you do?"
4. An inmate of the opposite sex leaves a love note under your plate when lunch is served in the employee snackbar?
5. A inmate who is not your orderly volunteers to clean up your area?
6. An inmate adjusts his or her clothing in front of you? e.g., pant zipper, belt, shirt buttons, undoing a few blouse buttons, etc.
7. An inmate asks you for a cigarette, pencils, or part of your lunch?
8. An inmate tells you a sexually suggestive story?
9. An article about an inmate appears in the local newspaper, and he asks you to bring a copy so he can read what was said about him?
10. An inmate tells you he has had a death in his family? He has no money to buy stamps. He has used his quota of free letters and wants you to drop a sympathy card into the mail box near your home.
11. You are alone making an inmate count, and you have ordered everyone to remain in place, yet one inmate refuses to obey?
12. An inmate says he has something extremely important to tell you: he mentions that you are the only officer he can trust, and that you must keep the information strictly confidential?

13. An inmate asks you about your personal life and how you handle your personal problems? He has indicated that he and his wife are having personal problems and financial difficulties.

14. An inmate of the opposite gender says, "How about going to bed with me?"

15. An inmate of the opposite sex has just been informed by prison authorities that the wife or husband, as the case may be, has been killed in an auto accident? The prisoner seems emotionally drained and through a torrent of tears requests a lock of your hair as a remembrance.

16. As a female officer, an inmate asks you to blot your lipstick on a piece of tissue and give it to him? No one will ever know and he has assured you he will never tell.

17. You discover that a former high school friend is an inmate working in your area of supervision?

18. As an officer you discover that a former boyfriend or girlfriend with whom you have had a sexual relation is now a prisoner in the institution where you work?

19. A former school chum is imprisoned in your institution: his parents want to visit your home frequently so you can keep them appraised of their son's progress?

20. You made a mistake in judgment and took a letter out for an inmate, and he now wants you to bring a package in to him that the mailman will deliver to your home? He threatens to expose the letter incident if you refuse.

21. An inmate offers you a gift he has made especially for you? He is your hard working, polite and respectful orderly; he spent much of his spare time in hobbycraft working on the moccasins for you.

22. You arrived home one evening and discovered three one hundred dollar bills in your coat pocket? The bills do not appear to be marked. You are having financial

problems and shared your dilemma with a few trusted inmates earlier that day.

23. An inmate asks you to step into a nearby equipment room because he has information regarding a cache of hidden weapons? He is afraid to discuss the matter openly because inmates may think he is a snitch. It could mean his death. He feels you are the only fair and trustworthy officer so he will not share with anyone else. Finding the weapons would make you look good in the eyes of a supervisor who recently criticized your performance.

24. An inmate has formed the habit of calling you by your first name?

25. An inmate says, "Can I ask you a personal question?"

26. An inmate exposes his genitals during count?

27. A former member of your church is a prisoner in your area of supervision, and he wants you to tell the minister to visit him?

28. An inmate frequently appears in your area for no valid reason or for reasons that are obviously false?

29. You are a staff member of the opposite gender and an inmate is being overly attentive to you? You do not appreciate the attention and want it stopped.

30. A prisoner berates a fellow officer in your presence for being given an inappropriate order and forced to carry it out?

Some Specific Answers

The time spent on this section of *Games Criminals Play* dealing with basic examples and explanations may appear excessive, even foolish, to the reader who has not experienced the prison environment. But these examples come from actual occurrences, and the unintentional, inappropriate responses of prison employees laid the groundwork for a set-up. An average college student may smugly think "I'm too smart for that," and some are. Yet, interestingly, in prison it is mostly college level people who become victimized by manipulators. This is not said to berate or degrade the person of knowledge. It is being said because most people working in today's prisons have had some college experience. Also, the authors realize many readers may well assume solutions to the situations related here only require common sense and simple reasoning because they are so basic. One may even conclude that people caught in a manipulator's trap have exuded a certain lack of reasoning power, but this is not so. Doctors, psychologists, teachers, and many other sophisticated professional people have been expelled in disgrace from correctional institutions for falling prey to fraudulent manipulators using one or several of the techniques discussed in this section. Why do these honest people become dishonest?

The reader must realize that most employees entering the correctional profession have lived their lives in communities surrounded by people of trust and reliability. In these close inner circles, a man's word is his bond, and they have come to expect and accept that philosophy as binding. Occasions upon which these community minded friends encounter cunningly dishonest criminals are by far the exception. Some may be cautious, but there is an inherent quality in mankind that hopes for honesty in all people. They tend to give the benefit of doubt, and shrug off the suspicion that someone would deceive them. In their desire to accept well-structured patterned information, subtle, hard-to-detect clues of manipulation escape them until it is too late. Now they realize that someone steeped in criminal thought has deceived them; that they have made some foolish mistakes; and that they must pay the consequences. P. T. Barnum once said, "A sucker is born every minute." A sucker is a person who is highly susceptible to the attractions of things specified, and in that person's naiveté, he or she will venture unsuspectingly into areas where even angels fear to tread. Like the professional described in the introduction to the questionnaire, judgment must be withheld until each reader has been exposed to coercion. Then, and only then, can labels such as "foolish" be attached when prison employees succumb to the pressure of manipulation that they face on a daily basis.

Described in the following pages are typical employee responses to the examples on the questionnaire. These are followed by appropriate responses and their reasoning. When matching your solutions, if you discover a propensity toward possible victimization, it does not mean you are unfit for a career in law enforcement. It does mean you should monitor your responses very closely in the actual criminal environment and constantly be aware of your own vulnerability.

Responses and Reasoning

The order of the responses and reasoning correspond numerically to those items in the Questionnaire.

1. Employee response to "I think you're beautiful."

    The employee encountering this situation was female. She responded with a slight blush and said, "thank you." The inmate approached her almost daily after issuing his first compliment, and his remarks became more and more brazen. The woman eventually sought aid from a supervisor who gave her the following advice . . .

    Appropriate response:

    "At the outset," the supervisor told her, "you should have said 'thank you for the compliment, but from this point on keep those kinds of opinions to yourself'." The supervisor further indicated that the situation was now out of control and it would be necessary to submit a general informational chrono of the type mentioned in the Protectors. "And," he said, "make sure the inmate gets a copy of the chrono. This brings everything in the open."

    Reasoning:

    Prison inmates who are bold enough to make remarks of this kind are usually strongly egocentric. They view women in corrections as being secretly succubae, and they strive to prove the concept as true. A "thank you" remark in the free community would be highly appropriate; however, in prison inmates will construe the reply to mean: she likes the attention and wants me to continue. She is in love with me, etc.

    The supervisor is advising a strict, business approach. The compliment is accepted and acknowledged in a polite business-like fashion, which conveys the admonition, "if you're sincere I'm grateful, but if you are not, I will tolerate no nonsense." Also, in prison circles, any inactive or silent response is interpreted as approval of one's actions.

2. Employee response to "I want your body."

Here the employee responded with embarrassment and the meek comment that the inmate should not be talking that way. The message she conveyed was that no action would be taken and she took no action. The inmate continued the comments in the belief that the woman wanted them continued. He was eventually locked up for grabbing her.

Appropriate response:

"I am not here to discuss my body, neither are you! I do not appreciate this kind of attention!" The incident should have been documented immediately with a copy sent to the inmate. The situation could have been stopped before it went any farther.

Reasoning:

In this situation the inmate is being excessively familiar and out of line. The business approach with a tone of harshness has the effect of discouraging future remarks that could be embarrassing to both parties. Inmates are fully aware of their expected conduct. They construe lack of command or inappropriate employee action as approval and plan their next move. Ninty-five percent of the time a female calls the shots. If she "turns an inmate on" she could suffer a tragic experience. Many inmates cannot stand rejection and will strike out at the person rejecting them. However, they do not consider it rejection when a situation is checked in its infancy. They do consider themselves rejected after hours of fantasying has created a false assumption.

3. Employee response to "no charge for nice officers."
   The employee accepted the inmate's offer and failed to pay for the meal.
   Appropriate response:
   Pay for the meal and report the inmate to his supervisor immediately.
   Reasoning:
   Acceptance of the favor caused both the employee and the inmate to be involved in the commission of a very serious rules violation, which eventually could result in isolation for the inmate and termination of employment for the staff member. This particular employee had developed a system of control based upon the "nice guy" image. He projected the style to an extent that caused him to lose control. When command tones were necessarily given, inmates would simply say, "Ah, come on, that's not like you!" And the employee would discontinue the effort. By accepting nonpayment of the meal, he had established a you/me situation which made it easy for both him and the inmate to continue the practice of illegal give and take. A condition now exists where the employee would be ashamed to share with his peers, and he has provided the inmate with a lever to use against him. In this case the inmate kept a very accurate account of the dollar amount and the number of meals not paid for. He ordered the staff member to bring in marijuana and threatened to expose the documents if he refused. The man complied for fear of losing his job. He was eventually caught and dismissed. The inmate's punishment was suspended since he cooperated with authorities during the investigation.

4. Employee response to the love note:
   The female employee destroyed the note and said nothing.
   Appropriate response:
   The note, together with a written report, should be forwarded to the inmate's supervisor immediately! A copy of the written report should go to the inmate.
   Reasoning:
   Here again is silent approval. The inmate reasoned that because the staff member took no action the note was appreciated, even desired. Tearing up the note demonstrated that she was protecting him by destroying the evidence. As time passed and the inmate encountered this employee in the institution corridors, he engaged in a series of touching incidents. Seemingly the touches were accidental at first, then obviously intentional. Again no action was taken. Finding the employee alone in an office one day the inmate asked for sex. The request was refused and the staff member brutally beaten.
5. Employee response to the offer of volunteer work.
   The staff member anxiously accepted the favor.
   Appropriate response:
   The employee should have said, "I'll check with your supervisor and if there are no objections to my utilizing this block of time, I will appreciate the help."
   Reasoning:
   This is a delicate situation. If the inmate is sincere, you would not want to insult him or accuse him of any wrong doing. If he is not sincere and is trying to make you feel obligated for accepting a favor, or to make it difficult for you to reprimand minor rules violations, you need to know. You do not want to

be the victim of a set-up.

If the inmate is sincere and really wants to keep busy, he will not mind if you ask his supervisor. As a matter of fact he will encourage it because sincere effort is appreciated by everyone. By speaking to the inmate's supervisor, you are keeping everything in the open. A you/me situation cannot be developed, and if the prisoner was intending to use the feeling of obligation to secure favors, he will object to the supervisional interaction and go in search of another victim.

6. Employee response to the inmate adjusting his clothing:
   The staff member appeared not to notice.
   Appropriate response:
   Order the inmate to be appropriately attired on every occasion when entering your area, and failure to comply will result in a report to the supervisor. Or, "This is not a dressing room—use the restroom if you need to make personal adjustments."
   Reasoning:
   Again, this is a testing process. Pretending not to notice indicates to the inmate that you cannot command or control; that you have a desire to view an exposed body; that a you/me situation is possible, and that you are desirous of the attention. This form of testing is based on the premise that the law of averages will eventually provide a victim. It may begin with an act as subtle as combing the hair—an act of preening oneself.

7. Employee response to small item request:
   Subject gave the inmate cigarettes.
   Appropriate response:
   I'm sorry, but there are rules against employees giving inmates their personal items.

Reasoning:

Giving cigarettes, pencils, or sharing lunches is a common practice of employees in corrections. Yet, research has shown that in almost every successful manipulation case, one of the first things requested and given is cigarettes. To even comment on the act would appear to the untrained observer as being "nitpicking." However, this is venturing into the realm of the familiar friendship. Remember professionals are unfamiliar friends.

8. Employee response to the off color story:

Whether the story is appreciated or not, so as not to embarrass the inmate most people respond by laughing as did the employee in this situation.

Appropriate response:

When you see where the story is leading, interrupt and say, "I'm sorry, but I don't appreciate those kinds of stories."

Reasoning:

Sex stories told by felons to male employees are designed to build a friendship bond so the employee will have difficulty saying NO, or calling attention to minor rules violations. Sex stories told to the opposite sex are frequently a testing process. The recipient's expression and body language are carefully studied for signs of approval. Once again, the idea is the law of averages will eventually provide a victim.

9. Employee response to the request for a local newspaper:

The employee brought the inmate a copy of the article.

Appropriate response:

"A copy of the paper is in the library, you can read it tonight after work." Or, "If my supervisor has no objections, I will bring you the article."

Reasoning:

Most inmates making this kind of request are not trying to manipulate. They are sincerely interested in the kind of publicity they are receiving from the press. However, in this situation the inmate created a you/me condition because the employee failed to ask the supervisor for permission to bring in the story. The inmate decided to see how many other items this staff member would bring him and he kept making requests for additional contraband. This continued until the employee had provided the inmate with a lever. The employee eventually reported the inmate, but was criticized for using poor judgment. It should be emphasized that it is not inappropriate to bring approved items to prisoners. But if you do, it is important to let the recipient know you obtained proper approval. By doing so, everything is in the open and the inmate will not entertain the thought that you violated rules to honor his request.

10. Employee response to the inmate professing a death in the family:

The employee felt sorry for the inmate and for weeks to come permitted minor rules violations: absence from work, sloppy workmanship and untidy room conditions.

Appropriate response:

First, check the story and make sure there was a death in the inmate's family. Once the truth has been determined, allow a reasonable amount of time for the inmate to be away from his duties. When he assures you he is ready to return, it is business as usual.

Reasoning:

Prisoners are not above creating conditions to test

124

your emotions. In one situation, an employee attempting to verify the death of an inmate's mother, found the woman very much alive and that the prisoner had used this same story on six earlier occasions. When finding a sympathetic employee, he would attempt to secure special favors to acquire a lever.

When prisoners experience a close personal tragedy in their lives, most prison employees make every effort to console, and most inmates appreciate and respect their concern. However, if in the throes of grieving he requests items or favors that are not customarily granted, he should be refused.

In the situation noted under employee response, the inmate did not have a death in the family. Through his earlier testing of this employee, he knew the staff member rarely verified information given him, and that he was still emotional over the recent death of his own sister. In cell discussions, other prisoners were convinced the officer would give special favors to anyone suffering a similar experience, so they elected the man's orderly to test their theory. The end result was a two week suspension for the officer because he gave his orderly two prescription sleeping pills.

11. Employee response to inmate refusing order to remain in place for count:

The situation did not seem threatening to the officer counting. She elected to continue the count, then acquired assistance and counselled with the inmate. She also submitted a report of the incident.

Appropriate response:

This was an appropriate response.

Reasoning:

The employee did not challenge the inmate's refusal

to obey orders because she was alone. Forcing the issue could have resulted in personal injury. However, the staff member did take action—it was just at a later time. The decision to gain assistance and counsel with the offender is a very professional approach. She correctly discerned that extenuating circumstances can alter behavior, and she wanted all possible evidence before finalizing her report. She discovered the inmate was in trouble with his peers, and they were going to stab him. The inmate's action was simply a way of drawing attention to himself so he could be placed in protective custody.

To the uninitiated free person, this inmate's approach may seem odd. One might say, "Why didn't the prisoner turn himself in instead of creating a scene?" In the criminal community, a man is expected to face death without saying a word; it's the "convict code." An inmate who knows he is in trouble with his peers may possibly find a way out if he does something to show strength and display disdain for the law. By acting out against authority, he has a chance for survival. But, the act of running or turning to "the man" for help is viewed as an unforgivable weakness and it seals his death warrant.

12. Employee response to confidential information offer:
    The employee promised confidentiality.
    Appropriate response:
    The inmate should be told that you will respect confidentiality under the following conditions:
    "I will not respect as confidential information anything that will adversely affect institution security, human life, the application of rules, and if your information deals with an area in which I have no expertise, I may discreetly seek advice from someone both of us can trust."

Reasoning:

Be careful of how you respond to requests for confidentiality because it could be a testing tool designed to create a you/me situation. If an inmate has a problem for which he is sincerely seeking a solution, i.e. home problems, sex pressure, etc., he will welcome your effort to aid him by consulting an expert in the field. If he wants to tell you the location of hidden weapons, drugs, or about inmates planning a killing, you have an obligation to enforce institution security and protect human life, which also includes your informant's. He should be told that you will share the information with trusted employees who will take care of the problem, and keep the informant's name confidential. Inmates wishing to manipulate a staff member will very often use confidentiality as a means of reading an employee's values. They may tell you of a stabbing that is to occur saying, "If you tell anyone, inmates will know I told, and instead of one killing there will be several." If you keep that information confidential and the stabbing occurs, the inmates now have a lever to use against you—concealing information leading to injury or death of a human being.

13. Employee response to inmate's request for personal information:

In this case, the employee discussed his financial status and intimate husband and wife relations with the inmate. The staff member felt he could control his area better if prisoners knew he could identify with their problems.

Appropriate response:

The inmate should be referred to his counselor or staff members who are hired and trained to deal with these kinds of problems. If problems are on the light side, an opinion may be expressed but should not contain any personal information.

Reasoning:

As you have seen in the study of a set-up, inmates who plan to victimize a person need this kind of information. An employee who controls at the expense of exposing personal problems creates a bond thereby making control, not easier, but more difficult. You can enforce rules with unfamiliar friends that are hard to enforce with familiar friends. Also, because people in confinement suffer a high level of complex emotional problems, the best help, if you sincerely wish to help them, is to refer them to personnel who are trained in these specific areas. Prisoners who are sincere in their request for help do not mind being referred to more capable sources; however, inmates plotting manipulation object to the reference suggestion very openly, pleading, "Only you can help."

14. Employee response to inmate's statement, "How about going to bed":

The employee elected to ignore the remark.

Appropriate response:

Cite the inmate for disrespect in a written report. Copies should go to the inmate, his file, your supervisor and the inmate's case worker.

Reasoning:

Remember, silence is construed by most prisoners as approval, and they will continue the pressure until some action is taken. As mentioned before, if you wait until the inmate believes his fantasies, rejection of his advances could mean danger to you.

15. Employee response to request for lock of hair:

In checking, the employee found the inmate to be truthful—a death had occurred in the family. Because the inmate seemed in a highly emotional state the employee granted the request.

Appropriate response:

(Politely, but firmly) "I'm sorry, but your request is against institution rules and my personal values."

Reasoning:

It is very difficult for some people to refuse an inappropriate request in light of a tragedy—especially when that request is made by the person who is suffering, and correctional employees are no exception. An inmate requesting entrance to an out-of-bounds area would be promptly denied, but an employee may very well permit the violation for someone who has just received a death notice. "The guy has had enough bad news for one day," is the reasoning. Prisoners are well aware of this human frailty, and manipulators use it to full advantage. Many levers are created during what employees feel is the inmate's hour of grief. It is sad to say, but many confined criminals have no feeling of grief over the demise of a family member. They act their sorrow for personal gain. The criminal's veil of honesty added to his hardship has caused many prison staff members to relax their control in an attempt to reduce a felon's suffering. Alert employees sympathize but do not bend the rules.

16. Employee response to request for lipstick blot:

In this situation the employee was ending a particularly difficult day, and did not feel she could handle one more confrontation. It seemed easier to blot her lips on a tissue and give it to the inmate. "After all,"

129

she reasoned, "what harm could it do?"
Appropriate response:
The prisoner should have been told in commanding
tones, "absolutely not," and the issue documented.
Reasoning:
This is not a normal request and it should have been
an indication to the staff member that she was dealing with a disturbed person, one who would misin-
terpret compliance of the request. The tissue became
a fetish for the inmate and, as his fantasies and day-
dreams increased in frequency, he became convinced
the woman was in love with him. He approached her
when she was alone intending to act out his dreams.
She resisted his advances and he lost all mental and
emotional control. The employee was rescued by
her peers just as the prisoner was about to strike her
with a chair. This situation would never have become
a distorted issue had the staff member refused and
documented the inmate's initial request. To save a
minute almost cost a life.

17. Employee response to high school friend now a prisoner:
The employee informed the prisoner that their former high school friendship could not be used as a
basis for special treatment, and then filed a written
report exposing the earlier relationship. A report
acknowledging prior knowledge of prisoners is required in many states.
Appropriate response:
This is an appropriate response.
Reasoning:
Everything was brought into the open. Ground rules
were established eliminating any possible thought of
using the former friendship as a means of securing
favors.

18. Employee response to inmate with whom a previous affair had occurred:

This staff member elected to conceal the earlier relationship by asking the prisoner to remain silent. The employee feared that knowledge of the affair would bring criticism from co-workers and supervisors.

Appropriate response:

Be very open. Discuss the situation with your supervisor and submit a written report indicating a close friendship and past knowledge of the prisoner.

Reasoning:

The employee's request for secrecy provided the inmate with a lever and created a you/me situation. This former boyfriend promised not to expose their earlier relationship, but there was a price for his silence. The staff member would have to once again provide the prisoner with sex. The attempt to conceal information about the relationship transferred control from the officer to the inmate. It assured eventual exposure, and caused unnecessary rumors about the affair to be circulated among staff and inmates. On the other hand, if proper reports had been submitted, the inmate would have been transferred to another section or to a different institution.

19. Employee response to parents' request for information about their son and visits to the officer's home:

The employee agreed.

Appropriate response:

The employee should have politely refused, told the parents to go through established channels, and reported the incident to his supervisor in writing.

Reasoning:

In this case the imprisoned son told his parents that unless he could provide marijuana to an inmate gang pressuring him he would be killed. Knowing his parents maintained a close relationship with the employee, he suggested use of the friendship as a means of getting the substance into the institution.

Professionalism can sometimes require the conversion of a familiar friendship to an unfamiliar one. The employee refused to smuggle in the drug which angered the parents, and bitter words severed the relationship. These problems would have been eliminated at the outset if proper reports had been filed and the parents placed in contact with their son's case worker or counselor.

20. Employee response to mistake in judgment—taking a letter out and inmate's marijuana request:

The employee complied. Inmates continued the pressure and eventually the staff member was caught and expelled from the institution.

Appropriate response:

Inform supervisors of the indiscretion and report the inmates.

Reasoning:

Here the employee has two choices: Report the mistake to administration and accept the better than average chance of retaining employment and reputation. Or, submit to inmate demands and lose all possibility of retaining employment and reputation.

Admitting a mistake is very difficult, but employers realize it takes a great deal of courage and honesty to do so. Most people try to be fair in their judgment. They know honest people profit from their mistakes and try not to repeat them. There is a strong possibility that disciplinary action will be minimal.

By submitting to inmate demands, the employee

will suffer great psychological damage and personality change in addition to risking the loss of job, family, friends and reputation. Here, disciplinary action will be maximum.

21. Employee response to inmate giving a gift:

The employee knew how hard the inmate had worked on the moccasins. He also knew the inmate had a fear of rejection, felt inadequate, and lacked confidence in his work. During construction of the slippers, the officer had praised the work hoping to build confidence in the inmate's ability to do this sort of work. He feared that refusal would throw the inmate into depression, so he placed the moccasins in his lunch box and took them home.

Appropriate response:

Praise for the finished product should be continued, and appreciation expressed for the gesture. Inform the inmate that by law you cannot accept gratuities; that you want them and you will immediately begin appropriate procedures to purchase them through the established channels.

Reasoning:

This inmate had an excellent institutional record and was sincere in wanting the officer to have the moccasins as a gift. Doing something good for someone who was appreciative was inwardly rewarding. However, he had been raised by parents who flaunted the law and criminal manipulation had become a life style. Knowing the officer had taken his gift without obtaining permission provided him with a lever to pressure for illegal contraband, but he mentally fought the idea because he liked the officer. His hedonistic desires overshadowed his better judgment because his life pattern of "doing the suckers" was too well established. He knew the officer could be made to feel sympathetic for someone in trouble so he began a running dialogue on his mother's poor financial situation. As time passed, the mother's problem accelerated and now she faced eviction for back payments on her home. The inmate needed $250. The officer refused and the inmate detailed his plan to expose the moccasin incident with the stern admonition, "Do as I tell you or you're out of a job!" The officer indicated his intent to comply, promising the money on the following day. The inmate informed the institution investigator that he was pressuring this staff member for money and suggested he observe the transfer from an isolated position in the housing unit. In the investigation that followed, the prisoner explained why he exposed the set-up. He stated he liked the officer and was dissatisfied with himself for giving in to the set-up temptation. He knew he would continue pressuring the employee and did not want to involve the staff member in additional crimes. He felt the best way out for both of them was to expose the plan.

22. Employee response when discovering three one hundred dollar bills in his coat pocket:

The staff member used the money to pay a bill.

Appropriate response:

Phone the institution immediately and report the incident.

Reasoning:

The employee erroneously thought the money could not be traced. He knew whoever placed the bills in his coat pocket would eventually approach him for favors, but felt he could handle the manipulator. The manipulators had developed an elaborate fool-

134

proof method of marking the money and forced the
employee into supplying them with marijuana. This
staff member was a well educated man who often
expressed his disdain for employees who place themselves in compromising situations. He had the mistaken idea that no "dumb con" could manipulate
him. He would boast, "In my eight years of teaching
inmates, I've been tried by the best and none was
successful."

23. Employee response to hidden weapon information:
The employee informed the prisoner that he would
discuss the matter with him in a more appropriate
place and that he would ask his supervisor to be present. He assured the inmate the supervisor could be
trusted and would respect the informant's concern
for confidentiality.

Appropriate response:

This was an appropriate response.

Reasoning:

A cautious correctional employee is aware that some
inmates are dangerous and could be leading them
into a trap. One-on-one situations should be avoided
as much as possible. Prisoners who state they trust
your judgment will continue in that trust when their
plans are changed. A prisoner who intends to harm
an employee will object violently at the suggestion
of a change.

Many employees in their zeal to impress a supervisor—particularly if that supervisor has criticized
them—have been harmed by placing themselves in
this kind of compromising position. There is no sub-
stitute for caution and inmates who are being sincere
respect a person's right to be cautious.

24. Employee response to using first names:

   The employee politely informed the inmate to use last names prefaced by the appropriate title such as Mr., or Officer, etc.

   Appropriate response:

   This is an appropriate response.

   Reasoning:

   Some prisons permit the use of first names if the employee and inmate agree. Yet in almost all successful set-ups, this kind of familiarity is evident at the outset. It is within the bounds of the familiar friendship and outside the bounds of professionalism. Some employees have last names that are difficult to pronounce. In these instances, employees permit the use of the first name preceded by the appropriate title, eg., Sgt. Bob, Ms. Sally, Officer Tom, etc.

25. Employee response to inmate wanting to ask a personal question:

   No, you may not!

   Appropriate response:

   This was an appropriate response.

   Reasoning:

   Because the employee rejected the inmate's request, he was somewhat stunned by her answer. Nevertheless he continued talking saying, "Would you read this to see if it would be objectionable to a woman?" The employee again rejected the request and the inmate apologized and left. In this situation the employee was a very attractive young school teacher. Inmates sought ways of presenting her with material written by them that expressed their sexual desires and feelings for her. Giving their expressions no encouragement, she appropriately rejected such nonsense because they did not relate to her class subject matter. Inmates were aware that if they needed aid in letter content and construction, she would assist them; and her approach, though polite, refused to acknowledge mediocrity. The teacher was astute enough to suspect inappropriate content of written material presented with the preface "personal" or the reference "woman."

26. Employee response to inmate exposing his genitals:

The employee, a woman, simply continued the count, giving no indication of shock or embarrassment. She later documented the behavior for action by appropriate authority and made sure the inmate received a copy.

Appropriate response:

This was an appropriate response.

Reasoning:

The inmate was testing this employee. He was attempting to distract her from counting. He was showing off to his peers by trying to embarrass the woman, and he was looking for attention. Her refusal to reenforce the behavior prevented a scene and deflated the ego of the prisoner. Her silence could not be construed as approval because she took action as soon as her count was completed.

27. Employee response to former church member requesting a message be carried to the minister:

The employee saw nothing wrong with the request, and told the inmate he would check with his supervisor. If the supervisor had no objections, the message would be delivered.

Appropriate response:

This was an appropriate response.

Reasoning:

Most correctional institutions encourage their staff

to take an active part in the rehabilitation process, but they want to know what the employee is doing. By informing the prisoner that his request would be processed through appropriate channels, two things are accomplished. First, the staff member has shown concern and a willingness to help the inmate find a better way of life. Second, by his obvious respect for rule enforcement and authority, he has set a good example and deterred any possibility of future use of a lever by the inmate.

28. Employee response to inmate in area for no valid reason: The inmate was not causing problems so the staff member said nothing.

Appropriaté response:

The staff member should have ordered the inmate to report to his job or his housing unit.

Reasoning:

In this case the inmate's action was a testing process to see how far he could push the rules before the employee would take action. By ordering the inmate out of the area, a clear message of command and control forestalls ideas of possible victimization.

Because of inaction on the part of prison personnel, inmates very often make wrong assumptions. Those assumptions can lead to unnecessary serious situations where one or both participants are punished or hurt. The point is this: immediate action prevents wrong assumptions and serious situations. Everyone, especially inmates, appreciate knowing where they stand. Preventing trouble beforehand is far easier and less dangerous than stopping trouble already in motion.

29. Employee response to over-attentiveness: The person involved in this situation began flirting

with staff of the opposite sex. The employee hoped the inmate would receive a message of unavailability to inmates.

Appropriate response:

The staff member should inform the prisoner that the attention is not appreciated, report the incident in writing to a supervisor and forward a copy to the prisoner.

Reasoning:

Most prison employees either underestimate or do not understand the criminal ego. When one attempts to send messages of unavailability by becoming overly attentive to one's peers, the prisoner will most often interpret the behavior as an attempt to make him or her jealous, and that the staff member really wants the attention. Women working in a male prison setting are especially prone to responding in this manner, and should be aware that this message sending will not be received as intended.

30. Employee response to prisoner berating staff:

As the prisoner berated the officer's poor behavior, the employee sided with the inmate.

Appropriate response:

Tell the prisoner that if he feels the officer's treatment techniques are wrong, he should politely discuss the matter with that staff member.

Reasoning:

By agreeing with a prisoner that one of your co-workers has acted inappropriately, a you/me situation is developed. Each person builds on the act of the other which fosters the prisoner's bitterness and could create a feeling in the inmate which goes from condemnation of officer's action to hatred. No worthy purpose is served when two people nurture discontent. If one staff member feels another has acted wrongly, he or she, like the inmate, should discuss the matter with that person. If the discussion results in an altered treatment approach, it would then be a matter of courtesy to jointly inform the prisoner of the new treatment technique. This type of action shows prisoners that staff is not closed minded, and it prevents future problems. Prisons have enough problems that develop naturally. Every effort should be made to avoid creating additional trouble.

Conversely, if a supervisor gives verbal reprimand to a subordinate that is overheard by an inmate who later attempts to console its recipient saying, "You didn't deserve that," etc., the employee should indicate to the prisoner that he is grateful for the concern but refuse to discuss the matter, because here again is an excellent foundation for a you/me situation. Someone has said, "Anger is just one letter from danger." Frayed emotions are difficult to deal with; the confined are aware of this and will use emotions as a we/they platform for coercement.

Having absorbed the information in this section and knowing what you should do about set-ups, what would you do if . . . ?

You are an academic math teacher. You have received permission from your supervisor to purchase at student expense, through a trust withdrawal, battery-operated hand calculators. You mention to the students that the shipment has arrived and you plan to pick up the calculators from the local vendor before the next session.

When class is dismissed, all inmates leave the room. Shortly one returns, shows you his calculator and says,

"Excuse me, Sir. I already have my own calculator; however, my batteries are dead. As long as you're going to be in the store to pick up your calculator purchase, would you mind picking me up a couple of batteries?"

Keeping in mind the importance of developing better staff/inmate relations, while at the same time establishing a platform of safety and control, how would you handle the situation?

PERSPECTIVE

Correctional facilities, houses of detention, or jails hire employees who possess natural strengths and talents administrators feel will benefit their individual institution treatment concepts. In the free society, these people can adapt their traits in ways deemed appropriate by the community but must exercise caution when applying them in the prison setting; a different pattern of social reasoning exists in the confined community. In other words, people who give of themselves freely and unselfishly outside of confinement are viewed as having strength of character, but prisoners may see these same people as potential victims for manipulation.

Paradoxically, it would appear that most of the difficulty employees get into when working in a prison is from their tendency to abuse their talents either by underuse or overuse. What many inmates characteristically refer to as weakness, limitations or shortcomings is often the employee's exaggerated use of their worthwhile strengths. In order for prison personnel to do their jobs, they must use their abilities productively and within the limits set by their employers. The excessive use of strengths, talents, traits or abilities creates a prison atmosphere and environment which makes relating to inmates difficult: it fosters hard rule pushing extremism on the one hand, or soft rule bending on the other.

141

Using the soft, mellow, and hard prisoner employee evaluation concept discussed earlier in this text, one can see the obvious reasons behind a set-up team's selection of a potential victim. The excessive life style—abuse of productive qualities by employees—will attract these team members as bees to honey.

TALENTS, TRAITS, ABILITIES, AND STRENGTHS

Excessively Soft	Productively Mellow	Excessively Hard
spineless	ADAPTABLE	unrelenting
paternal	HELPFUL	demanding
slavish	LOYAL	restrictive
permissive	OPTIMISTIC	impractical
inconsistent	SEEKS EXCELLENCE	perfectionistic
submissive	SUPPORTIVE	indifferent
gullible	CAUTIOUS	suspicious
pretentious	AMBITIOUS	ruthless
solicitous	COMPETITIVE	combative
obligatory	FORCEFUL	dictatorial
lenient	ORGANIZED	rigid
impulsive	QUICK TO ACT	rash
self-conscious	SELF-CONFIDENT	arrogant
docile	TENACIOUS	obstinate
careless	ANALYTICAL	nit-picking
capricious	FAIR	unfeeling
vacillating	FIRM	inflexible
overfamiliar	FRIENDLY	sectarian
obsequious	PRINCIPLED	purist
easily distracted	THOROUGH	obsessive

The mellow person—according to the prisoners—is a professional; the soft-person is easily manipulated; and the hard

142

person is covering a weakness, thus is easily manipulated. This is not to say the mellow person cannot venture into the extremities of his or her qualities occasionally, but it is to say one must be careful in so doing. The helpful, mellow person may find it advantageous to be paternal in one situation or demanding in another to accomplish a worthy purpose; but, to be totally paternal or totally demanding is opening oneself up to coercement. There is an adage, "You can't keep a bird from flying over your head, but you can keep him from building a nest in your hair," and many others that confirm the Biblical admonition to use moderation in all things. Exaggerated use of one's talents, traits, abilities, or strengths is usually counter-productive, whereas moderation proves productive. Correctional employees, in order to be professional, cannot be extremists because this eventually fosters dissatisfaction, disillusionment, bitterness, and malcontent. Moderation produces satisfaction, creativity, desire to achieve, and mellowness. When monitoring their own actions and responses in the confined community, employees must consider all of their productive qualities—the inmate will.

Backlash

The sections in this book on The Set-Up, Protectors, and A Questionnaire with Answers were designed to provide the reader with a means of recognizing a set-up and preventing or stopping one. Recognition of a set-up occurs when a person of reasonable judgment identifies its steps. Prevention of a set-up happens when that person learns to isolate and change personality traits that convey a message of susceptibility to manipulation and analyzes words and actions in advance of their usage to avoid all possibility of misinterpretation. Messages of vulnerability cannot be received if no message is emitted. Recognition and prevention of a set-up causes little, if any, adverse reaction between manipulators and their intended victims because the possibility and hope of rewards have not been firmly established. On the other hand, stopping a set-up is quite different.

To say "stopping a set-up" implies that one is in progress;

144

it is being developed. The practitioners believe in the possibility of success and the hope of achievement. A set-up in progress represents a substantial investment in their time and emotion. Manipulators believe they possess a vested interest in a program that will pay dividends. They protect their investment and react unpredictably when some unexpected intervention prevents the possibility of profit. When this blockage occurs, disappointment turns to resentment and, with the loss of their objective gain, a vindictive backlash of threats and invectives can be expected by the principals causing the loss. Consider the following case.

In frequent discussions with a prison employee, a correctional lieutenant became uneasy over some of the things that his friend indicated inmates were saying and doing. He began researching files of inmates most frequently mentioned by the employee and discovered that one of them had been involved in a situation at a different prison where an employee was dismissed for supplying inmates with drugs. In mentioning this to his friend, he further discovered the employee had developed a strong friendship with the inmate in question and had provided him with a series of inappropriate favors. This had been going on for over six months. In discussing this employee's performance with other supervisors, the lieutenant found a consensus indicating an inability to control. "A specific group of inmates," they said, "were taking him for a ride." Further investigation revealed this staff member had permitted an inmate to make a series of unauthorized phone calls, provided him with two cartons of cigarettes, and failed to report an incident where the inmate struck one of his peers. The lieutenant felt the employee was capable of controlling inmates; that if his friend could be made to realize inmates were manipulating him, he could overcome his mistakes; and that the time to bring everything into the open was NOW!

145

After seeing the total picture and agreeing with the lieutenant that he was being victimized, the employee filed reports giving names and details of situations where inmates requested illegal contraband, and of the fight that had not been reported. He admitted to his own mistakes, and in the presence of the lieutenant, he verbally reprimanded the inmates involved. The exposure brought the set-up to a prompt conclusion. In the days that followed, the exposed set-up participants subjected the employee to a variety of harrassments—threatening notes, cold icy glares, and profane degrading remarks—as he passed them on the yard.

Backlash is a style of psychological torture that can continue for months. During this time, the employee can become fearful and apprehensive so peer support is essential. In this backlash stage, striking out is mostly verbal and psychological. Prisoners rarely harm a person they had attempted to victimize, but caution should be exercised at all times because it has happened. Interestingly, while the unsuccessful set-up team is engaged in backlash, other teams will test that group's victim. It is a method of assuring that the individual can control, and an attempt to prove that "where your group failed, mine can succeed."

Sometimes staff gives its own kind of backlash. And although it is not usually intended to be cruel, the employee may have to take some derisive teasing about being a "duck." As the employee shows improved skills, the unwanted staff attention quickly fades into respected acceptance.

As time passes, the former victim gains in confidence and becomes less and less apprehensive. He or she will continue to help inmates in their struggle for rehabilitation, but a new dimension has been added to their command techniques. It is a sophistication gained only through experience that shows strength of character and personal pride. The attribute is easily detectable, very professional, and devoid of vindictiveness. Backlash usually has the effect of aiding professional skills rather than detracting from them—even though it is hell to go through.

The staff member who stopped his set-up found this to be true. He discovered that in order to prevent giving inmates messages of vulnerability, he would have to evaluate personality traits that were giving false messages. He decided that these traits could be improved upon or changed without loss of identity. He knew he found it easier to look the other way rather than address a conflict or minor rules violation. He knew he was not fond of details and tended to overlook signs giving clues of impending trouble. And he knew he accepted inmate advice without checking its validity and did favors for inmates that he was ashamed to share with his peers.

As this staff member began addressing conflicts immediately, became more detail oriented, observed the minor along with the major rules, and became more open with his dealings with inmates, he was surprised to find that both inmates and staff respected his ability to perform his duties. Although inmates continued to test him, the employee was now able to recognize and prevent set-ups. Along with this staff member's newly acquired approach came greater job enthusiasm, improved treatment skills, and a deeper sense of self-esteem.

Case
Histories

CASE HISTORY I

Profile—Staff Member

Subject is a thirty-four year old female Caucasian with less than one year correctional experience. She is attractive, ambiverted, and friendly. Her profession is academic teacher and reading specialist. She has a Master's Degree, and is considered proficient and capable as an instructor. Her personality is stable and her pleasant, friendly classroom approach is seen as an asset. She is the mother of four children, and an active member in community affairs. Throughout this presentation she will be referred to as Mrs. Chase.

Profile—Prison Inmate

Subject is a tall, thin, white male about twenty-eight years of age, with a lifetime history of acting out in a criminal fashion. He suffers minor brain damage from excessive use of drugs, and his prognosis for change is poor. His long experience of being in and out of prisons has made him "con-wise" and he is able to appear trustworthy and desirous of improving his former life style. He has been assigned to Mrs. Chase as a teaching assistant, and he will be referred to as Inmate Wilson.

Setting

The setting is an academic high school classroom in a California prison. Prison school rooms are usually designed so that instructors are clearly visible to security staff. However, in this instance, the room had only one window and included a back area for books and files. Anyone working in that area would be completely obscured from view by the divider. Also, the reader should be aware that inmate teaching assistants are very often alone with the teachers in these classrooms for periods of from one to two hours a day.

To further establish the setting, let's assume that you are Mrs. Chase. You are outgoing and friendly, possess a trusting nature, and have a desire to help people find a better way of life through education. You are about to begin your first semester of teaching prisoners and you are a little apprehensive. Your only knowledge of the criminal society came from a forty-hour orientation program designed for new employees. But you are not too concerned, because in the past you've had to maintain classroom control over some very difficult students. "Inmates," you think to yourself, "couldn't be much different. People are people regardless of where you find them."

Your past experience has taught you that a pleasant attitude, individual attention, and a little understanding and kindness are the keys to developing good citizens. You are convinced that if these techniques work outside a prison, then there's no reason why they shouldn't work inside one. You are confident of your ability to handle almost any situation. On the surface everything is as you expected it to be, so you are anxious to begin the semester. Still, you are curious.

This description could fit any number of teachers hired by the Department of Corrections. However, this one is a profile of an academic instructor whom inmates selected to be the victim of a set-up. At the outset the reader should be aware that Mrs. Chase suspected that she was being victimized, and reported her suspicions to the prison authorities. She was instructed to report all inmate activities and attention given her, and told that as soon as evidence could be obtained substantiating her suspicions, the inmates involved would be arrested. Her teaching assistant and her students were closely observed, and experienced staff members agreed that she had been selected as the proposed victim of a compromise.

Mrs. Chase is one of the few victims of a set-up who was able to observe the process unfold and almost attain maturity without being harmed, or without having suffered the loss of her job. Even though she knew she was being victimized, there were times she doubted the process was real. "The acting, the sincerity and the subtle, very believable situations presented," she said, "were convincing enough to make me believe that the inmates had my best interest at heart."

As this case is developed, it will be broken into sections showing each phase of the set-up. These steps are usually intermingled and separating them without losing the slow, subtle approach is at best difficult. Total time involved was six months.

The Observation Step

In order to get to her classroom, it was necessary for Mrs. Chase to cross the main prison recreation yard. As she proceeded to her area, inmates would subject her to a series of "cat calls." Being the only female instructor, she had formed the habit of walking with her male counterparts, and

150

when she heard the calls, she would jokingly say to one of the men, "Inmates are calling to you again." Inmates, being unable to hear her comments, interpreted her slight smile and slight hint of embarrassment as being appreciative of the attention. Once in the educational area, inmates appeared friendly and sociable.

At this particular institution, teachers are permitted to interview and select their own inmate teaching assistants. Mrs. Chase selected Inmate Wilson because she had observed him in a prison college class, and felt he was capable of performing teaching assistant duties. She summoned Wilson for an interview and offered him the job. "Do you really want me?" he asked. Her affirmative response caused him to surmise that she liked him, and he placed greater importance on the relationship than she had intended. He made this assumption because Mrs. Chase had expressed concern for him when he engaged in a series of self "put-downs" as a result of a speech he had made at his prison college class.

On a personal level, he told her of his observations—of her nervousness, "You tighten up when you walk the yard; but you seem okay in the education area," and of her manner of dress—"You seem more lively when you wear bright colors than when you wear your drab clothes. I really like your yellow outfit."

At lunch time, Mrs. Chase ate in the employee snack bar serviced by inmates. When taking her order, or when serving the meal, they would address her using her first name. She voiced no objection. This group also listened to her conversations as she talked with other employees. Since staff at this institution don't like to discuss "shop talk," inmates were able to pick up her likes and dislikes, her biases and interests. These were reported to her teaching assistant and other members of the set-up team by the observers.

151

Selection of a Victim

In the days that followed his selection as teaching assistant, Wilson subjected Mrs. Chase to all phases of the observation process and formed the opinion that she was deeply interested in his welfare, that she was a woman of deep and profound emotions, that she leaned toward the "underdog," and that her feelings for him exceeded the normal bounds of friendship. Team members surmised that she was friendly, warm and naive. They were aware that she was a new employee and assumed that her lack of experience with prisoners would make her an ideal set-up candidate. To test these theories, Wilson enlisted the help of friends, and situations were set up to confirm or deny the assumptions.

Test of Limits, and/or "Fish Testing"

Wilson invited his friends to visit the classroom on occasions when no other students were present to see if Mrs. Chase would allow the visitations. These inmates had previously worked for her, and even though they were not assigned to her class, they volunteered to help her organize and clean her new room. Because they had performed what they considered to be favors, it was felt she would have difficulty turning them away. Having proved this theory correct, the visits became more and more frequent. Also, conversations during these visits attested that Mrs. Chase was indeed a warm, overtly friendly person who had a desire to help prisoners become better citizens.

At this point the set-up team incorporated the use of a runner. His task was to ask for small items at first, and larger items later, if his first requests were honored. He was promised payment in drugs. The runner's first request was for school materials. Because he was not a student, Mrs. Chase refused. He later approached her on the yard as she was going to class and requested a cigarette. She gave him one. When Mrs. Chase informed authorities of the transaction, she was told that he would approach her again the following day and each day thereafter until she refused. Acting on this advice, she refused his next request with the admonition that a disciplinary report was in the offing if he continued to bother her. He tested her again by just visiting sporadically after a few weeks, then made another request; she did not report him as she indicated, so the tests continued.

Other inmates involved in this set-up conducted other types of tests and they will be discussed under the headings to which they applied. It should also be noted that the set-up team members were not strangers to Mrs. Chase. They had worked for her at an earlier time.

It was at this stage that Mrs. Chase told authorities that she thought she was being "cultivated."

Support System

Mrs. Chase was complimented on a rather frequent basis by members of the set-up team, but most frequently by her teaching assistant, Inmate Wilson. On one occasion he said to her, "I've never said this to anyone else in my life, but you are the best teacher I've ever seen. You're not like these other instructors, you explain things so they are understandable." Other members of the group complimented her abilities as a teacher, the condition and decor of her room, and they volunteered to mop and wax her floors. Anything she needed was appropriated, such as more electrical outlets: Inmate Wilson provided the work request, drawn-up plans, and immediate installation by inmates once the plans had been approved by supervisors. Inmate Wilson appeared enthusiastic and dedicated to his job. He was always prompt and made sure that all the mundane paper work was completed. He helped create a filing system and processed all ordered material. And, although Mrs. Chase kept her finger on the paper work, it was convenient to let the efficient teaching assistant process it. All she had to do was teach.

The support system is on-going. Everyone enjoys a compliment, and inmates know how to give them. So, from the beginning of a set-up to the point where the victim suspects something is wrong, this kind of support is offered.

The Plea for Help

Since everything was kept up to date by the teaching assistant, preparation time was sometimes free for discussions.

"I don't know why you bother with me, Mrs. Chase. I've been a failure all my life, I have no confidence in myself, and that speech I made was really bad. You would be fighting a lost cause, but I need your help," Wilson told her during one of their alone periods.

Mrs. Chase refused to allow him to wallow in self-pity, saying, "You're wrong, you are a capable person, the speech you made was excellent! If the work you produce outside of prison is as good as your work here, you can do anything anyone else can do. What you need to do is to stop feeling sorry for yourself, and stand on your own two feet."

"And I want to do that," Wilson said, "but I'm not sure I know how. Maybe, if you're willing to work with me, I can get over these feelings of inadequacy. A lot of people have tried to help me in the past and got nowhere, but I really believe that you could do it. I have a great deal of faith in you."

Mrs. Chase indicated that she would be willing to help in any way she could, but that the bulk of the effort would be his to shoulder.

As time passed, Mrs. Chase and Inmate Wilson had many conversations of this nature. Wilson began to construe her attention toward him as becoming emotional and perhaps even sensual. Mrs. Chase, on the other hand, had no such feelings, and being new to the prison environment, was not aware that her attention could be construed in this manner.

Practitioners of set-ups learn to become aware when a particular phase of their operation is wearing thin, and Wilson began to suspect he had taken self-pity as far as it would go. Through this phase he had learned a great deal about Mrs. Chase's feelings and emotions. He was relatively certain that he knew the types of things that would deepen the relationship he felt was developing. "It is time," Wilson thought, "to go on to other things."

Empathy and/or Sympathy

The friendship between Mrs. Chase and her teaching assistant had grown to where they shared on a more personal level. They talked about their families, financial matters, and personal problems encountered through living. In other words, they empathized. Mrs. Chase had been divorced, and Wilson was having problems with his girlfriend. The things that had happened in Mrs. Chase's life Wilson could identify with because he had had similar experiences. These similarities have the effect of forming a bond between two people because each can understand what the other had been through. When two people undergo a divorce there is a lot of heartbreak. There is also a tendency for a person who has been through this process to console someone in the throes of it. Very often the consoling is demonstrative. Wilson understood this human feature. He felt that Mrs. Chase would feel deeply sorry for him if he had such a problem, and he hoped she would demonstrate her sorrow.

One day he said, "I don't know what to do. My girlfriend sent me a letter saying she's leaving me. I even had a child by her. I love her and I love that baby. I'll go crazy if I lose them. Besides, the baby is a bleeder and I'll go out of my head wondering if something has happened, and never be able to know. I don't know what's wrong with me. It seems like everything

I touch turns to dirt!"

Mrs. Chase's heart went out to him. As he suspected, she was sorry for his experience, but there was no physical demonstration. She told him, "These things are always very difficult, especially for you because you're in confinement. I truly wish I could help you."

Once again Mrs. Chase reiterated her earlier statement that this was a time for him to display his manly strength and stand on his own two feet. He assured her he would try, but implied he might need her help. She understood. Because of her concern for him, Wilson felt that the relationship had deepened even more.

As the days passed, Wilson was able to maintain his composure. He did, however, have an occasional relapse which required some deep discussions. But for the most part he handled the situation quite well. He also managed to maintain a line of communication that supplied information about the baby. Wilson was able to use his estrangement as a means of gaining sympathy for two or three weeks before it began to outlive its usefulness.

In the meantime, Mrs. Chase was given a training assignment that kept her away for several days. She returned to find Wilson in an extremely emotional state of anxiety. "What's the matter?" she inquired.

Wilson found talking difficult and almost lost his composure. "While you were gone," he said, "my baby passed away. I loved that child. You can't live with, protect, and nurse a child that's a bleeder without developing a very special kind of love." Mrs. Chase was deeply concerned. She consoled him as best she could, but what can one say to someone suffering such a close personal loss?

Wilson continued his rendition of the facts, as he understood them, that led to the baby's death. He said, "I feel so helpless, so confined, and I can't even apply for a temporary community leave to attend the funeral."

Mrs. Chase was confused; she knew that prisoners could be released long enough to take care of such emergencies. "Why can't you go?" she asked.

"I can't attend and see my child one last time because I have enemies in that area of the state that have pledged to kill me," he told her.

Authors' Note: Even though Mrs. Chase had been told by authorities that she was being primed for a compromise situation, and she had been reporting the activities of the set-up team, she began to wonder if her staff contact was advising her correctly. When reporting the baby's death, she said, "I would really like to believe, but Inmate Wilson's expressions, his emotions, and his sincerity were very real. I don't believe a person could act that well." Authorities assured her that the child was not dead, and that this situation was all part of a plan leading to a request for favors. She returned to her classroom with feelings of doubt.

Each day for two or three weeks after Wilson had informed Mrs. Chase of the baby's death, he had periods of depression. He felt guilty over not attending the funeral, and he was remorseful because he had been such a poor father. He sought her assurance that he was capable of carrying on in life. When Mrs. Chase submitted her next report, she indicated her belief that Wilson was not being deceptive. "I believe," she said, "that the baby really died. His states of depression are too real, and he has been writing notes indicating that he intends to take his own life."

Once again her staff contact gave the assurance that the child was alive. He also told her that the suicide notes were only for her eyes, and that the inmate's intent was to elicit an overt emotional response from her. Again, Mrs. Chase wanted desperately to believe her staff contact, but doing so required effort. In order to give Mrs. Chase a more valid assurance that

Wilson was being deceptive according to a prescribed plan, her staff contact outlined the steps of a set-up and told her what Wilson had in mind for his next operational phase.

Allusions to Sex

"While preying on your sympathy, Wilson will now begin making references to sex," her staff contact told her. "He believes that your feelings for him are so deep that you will allow that taking of this liberty; and that if you do he will be convinced that you wish his physical attention."

Mrs. Chase displayed very little response to this admonition. She seemed deep in thought and changed the subject.

The following day Inmate Wilson called Mrs. Chase's attention to a certain inmate and said, "Watch out for that fellow, he's a sleaze. He came to my living area last evening and asked if I was 'getting any' from you." Having made the statement and observed her reaction, he quickly assured her that he had promptly put the inmate in his place, and that he knew she was not that kind of person. Mrs. Chase elected not to react to or give Wilson's allusion to sex the attention he expected, and she began to realize that Wilson might not be sincere in the "nice guy" image that he was trying to project.

When a set-up reaches this stage, it is a common practice of inmates to space their references to sex. They must allow some time to pass so the victim doesn't become suspicious. The victim is distracted from dwelling on the sex allusion by pledges of support and we/they conversations.

The We/They Syndrome

"You know, Mrs. Chase, we think they gave you the worst room in the school. You really keep it looking nice, but a teacher with your capabilities should be treated better than this." Several different members of the set-up team made statements like this to Mrs. Chase. They attempted to seed the thought that the administrators were not treating her as they should. Once the idea of unfairness from supervisory staff is tried, the process is further developed by making the victim feel that other, less capable teachers are getting far better consideration from administration. On one occasion Wilson indicated that Mrs. Chase shouldn't be made to feel subservient to the school office secretary, that several of the teachers didn't maintain upkeep on their classrooms as well as Mrs. Chase, yet they had the better rooms. Mrs. Chase told them she didn't buy this.

Inmate Wilson had also observed an occasion when Mrs. Chase reported the actions of an unruly inmate to her supervisor and he took no action. Mrs. Chase was uncomfortable with this inattention, so Wilson suggested that they (administration) were not concerned with her welfare, that she was being treated like an inmate, but that she didn't have to worry because he would not allow inmates to act out in her classroom.

Offer of Protection

Very early in this set-up process Mrs. Chase had some difficulty controlling black inmates. She ordered one of them to behave himself or leave the room. He refused at first, called her a bitch, then did as he was told. Her teaching assistant promptly informed her that inmates like this were in the majority at this institution, and that if he were not around she could be harmed. He then volunteered to escort her wherever she went. "Is that O.K. with you?" he asked.

She stated, "Do whatever makes you feel comfortable." So Wilson became her escort and protector.

The offer of protection is an extremely important phase of a set-up. The situation described above provides an opening for the offer, but the connotation is obliging. The victim must be made to feel the need for protection. She must desire it, and be grateful for receiving it. Instilling this kind of feel-

159

ing in the victim is not easy. It must be done with great care, so the victim suspects nothing. This is usually a staged event and it incorporates the use of fear.

Mrs. Chase was alone in her room during a break one morning when an unassigned inmate entered her room, seated himself where his actions could be clearly observed, and began rubbing his groin in a highly suggestive manner while inquiring about her new class. She told him to leave. Mrs. Chase was not aware that this was part of the testing process, that she was being observed for her reaction, or that this inmate was acting under orders from her teaching assistant. She reported the incident to her supervisor and he took no action. This provided Inmate Wilson the opportunity of reiterating his offer of protection. He knew that Mrs. Chase felt uneasy and alone, especially since staff action was nonexistent. He said, "I wish I had been here, that never would have happened. There is no doubt in my mind that if given a chance a guy like that would harm you."

As mentioned at the beginning of this case history, the room which was assigned to Mrs. Chase had an area where she could be obscured from the view of the custodial staff. That area, or back room, provided Wilson with the tool he needed for the instillation of fear. He continued his conversation, "Do you realize that one of these crazy inmates could force you into that back room, and neither your whistle nor your screams could be heard? But don't worry, I won't let that happen."

The offer of protection was completed. It was needed and necessary, and Mrs. Chase was comforted, knowing that Wilson would look out for her welfare. Little did she realize that in the set-up plan Wilson was going to be the inmate to force her into the back room.

160

The Touch System

The same day that Wilson made the offer of protection, he was certain that Mrs. Chase's feelings for him would allow the touching process to begin, but he still must remain cautious. His ultimate goal was to request sexual favors, and he felt she had responded properly to all the phases, and that in the final analysis, she would grant his request. He still realized that he could be wrong in his interpretation of her responses. He was anxious, but not anxious enough to expose his intentions. That evening, as Mrs. Chase prepared to leave the classroom, he began the touching process by adjusting her blouse collar. "That's been bothering me all day," he said. He theorized that if she had no objections—and she voiced none—he would advance the touch system in the evenings to follow.

Mrs. Chase had been advised that the touch system in some form was next. When it actually happened, she froze as a cold chill of fear went down her spine, and she couldn't say a thing.

The Lever

The lever, as you recall, is some type of rules' violation that can be used to threaten or coerce a staff member into bringing in contraband or providing inmates with favors. The lever in Mrs. Chase's case was established very early in the set-up. She began her career in corrections as an intermittent teacher, and as such moved from classroom to classroom. During this time most of the inmates involved in the attempt to compromise her had been her students, and they had assisted her in a variety of classroom cleaning tasks. When she attained permanent status, and was assigned her own room, they again performed such functions as washing and waxing floors, rearranging furniture, etc. Also, the reader should keep in mind that teachers were permitted to give prisoners a variety of school materials, but no one bothered to outline to Mrs. Chase which ones were permissible.

She had ordered four drawing pencil sets from state supplies, and only two sets arrived. Because they were a necessary teaching tool, she augmented her supply by purchasing two sets out of her own funds. Two of these former students were engaged in drawing projects, so she loaned a set to each of them. She was not aware that this particular item was not to be given out, plus she made the mistake of telling these inmates that she had purchased and brought them into the institution. The set-up team now had a lever to use against her when the time came for them to demand favors.

Use of the lever is a simple process. For example, each phase of a set-up is designed to establish an overly-familiar relationship with the proposed victim. The theory is that when favors are requested, they will be granted because it is difficult to refuse a friend. If it develops this way, then use of the lever or force is not necessary. If the request is refused, the victim is reminded that he or she introduced illegal contraband into the institution; if this evidence is produced, the employee's service will be terminated. If the victim still refuses, and, depending on how desperately the favor is desired, the employee may undergo force.

Mrs. Chase was not subjected to the last three phases, i.e., use of the lever, the shopping list, and use of force because the authorities felt the following circumstance broke the anticipated pattern and fine line of the set-up and they could not predict or control the new circumstances to obtain "hard evidence against the inmates." They advised her to relieve the teaching assistant of his duties immediately, which she did.

The circumstances are as follows: One Friday afternoon the school administrator informed Mrs. Chase, in front of Inmate Wilson, that he intended to change her room and monitor the students attending her classes, and that this change would develop after the week-end. Wilson was now forced to accelerate the set-up plans, so he decided to skip the remaining phases and make his demands. With the aid of team members, a prison-made knife was placed in a book in the back room. He planned to wait until she went into the area, then he would follow and request sexual favors. If she refused, he would acquire the knife and her choices would be to submit or be stabbed—perhaps even killed.

Fortunately, the plan was not allowed to materialize.

The backlash lasted over a year—until four members of the set-up team paroled, and three were transferred.

CASE HISTORY II

Profile—Staff Member

Subject is a twenty-nine year old Caucasian of medium build. He is a Supervising Cook I and has eight years' experience working in correctional institutions. He is known to be racially prejudiced, with a particular hatred for Blacks. His work record is good, but it is suspected that many of his disciplinary reports against Black inmates have no basis in fact. He is married, has two children, and answers to the name of "Phil."

Profile—Prison Inmate

Subject is a twenty-three year old Caucasian named "Harry." He is incarcerated for the crime of grand theft, and is considered by institutional authorities to be a gang leader. His work pattern is inconsistent and sporadic, and he has been known to encourage inmate sit-down strikes. He is not well educated, but is considered "con-wise." Subject displays symptoms of a psychopath, cannot work in harmony with other people, and does not profit from his mistakes.

The Set-Up

"The state's damned affirmative action plan has done it to me again!" Phil said to one of his peers. "I work like hell for a promotion, and what do they do? They give it to a Black. They've gone from one extreme to the other. No one felt it was right when the Blacks were kept down; well, what about the Whites? I shouldn't be held back because of the color of my skin."

Having just received notice of a zero oral interview for a promotional step that he wanted, Phil was bitter. He was expressing himself in loud tones without regard to who was listening. Several inmates overheard Phil venting his feelings,

164

and eventually one of them engaged him in conversation.

"I know just how you feel," the inmate said. "It's because of the Blacks that I'm in jail."

Phil regarded the inmate closely for a moment, then inquired, "What makes you say that?"

The inmate continued, "I was a cook on the streets. I lost my job and went to look for another. Each time I interviewed for a position, they wound up hiring a minority. Blacks are taking over the cooking profession out there on the bricks (streets)."

"That's true," Phil said, "but what's that got to do with your going to prison?"

The inmate looked at Phil as if he couldn't believe the question. "That's not hard to figure out," he told Phil. "If you don't work, you don't eat. I had a wife and two kids to support. I couldn't let them starve, and if all the jobs are going to the Blacks, there's nothing left to do but steal. Right?"

"Well, I'll be goddamned," Phil said, and as he continued to talk he became enraged. "Affirmative action has sunk to a new low. Now they're causing people to go to prison. By the way, what's your name?"

"Harry," the inmate responded.

"Well, Harry, you can call me Phil. We White boys have to stick together. I guess that's the only way we're going to beat this thing."

Phil didn't know it, but his prejudice and hatred for Blacks had just caused him to be selected as the victim for a set-up.

Of all the diseases in the world, hatred is one of the worst, and has probably destroyed more people than any other affliction. Inmates schooled in street psychology are well aware of the destructive power of hatred, and they are quick to cultivate the animosity if it can work to their best advantage.

Harry was not an educated man, but he was smart enough to know that two men in exact agreement of a hatred feed each other's egos, and that a special bond is formed. The world-against-you-and-me attitude opens the doorway to empathy, sympathy and all other aspects of a set-up.

A bond formed out of prejudice must constantly be fed, so Harry supplied Phil with daily examples of how affirmative action was causing the White man to lose his identity, and Phil reciprocated with his own repertoire of bombastic material.

It wasn't long before Harry told Phil of an article that he had heard of in a somewhat radical publication that expressed views similar to their own. "Inasmuch as you are on the streets," Harry said, "why don't you pick up a copy, and we can read it together?"

Harry had been testing the friendship bond between the two of them. He noticed that when Phil assigned kitchen duties to other inmates, he gave special consideration to Whites. Also, when inmates were reprimanded for laziness, nothing was said to him, and he was the worst of the lot. So he was relatively certain that Phil wouldn't mind his request for the magazine.

The article was everything they hoped it would be. They discussed the information, nurtured their hatreds, and agreed to one day do something about the Black situation in America. As they read and shared their opinions, it seemed that Harry was always out of cigarettes and found it necessary to "bum" from Phil. During one of their conversations, Harry said, "Would you lend me a package of cigarettes until I can get to the canteen? I hate to be asking all the time. I'll have money on the books soon and be able to pay you back." Phil placed little importance on the request, and gave him the cigarettes. Harry also asked if he could take the magazine article with him to share with some friends. "I'll return it to you," he said.

166

Phil's response was, "Fine, go ahead."

Sometime later, Harry called Phil's attention to yet another article on Blacks, only this one was in a very heavily radical publication, and Phil was in doubt as to whether or not he should buy it.

"We don't care about all the other trash in those magazines," Harry said. "We may be prisoners, but we're loyal Americans. Loyal enough," he continued, "to want to get rid of the Blacks." That was all Phil needed. He bought the magazine and, like the other one, he loaned it to Harry.

When 'Harry displayed this publication, other inmates wanted to know where he got it. He answered, "From Phil, the supervising cook."

"What's he doing with a magazine like that?" they asked.

"Didn't you know?" Harry looked surprised, "Why that guy's a radical son-of-a-bitch!"

The thought was seeded, and the rumors began to fly. As more and more inmates told the story, it became very distorted, and Phil—according to this rumor—was a former storm trooper from the American Nazi Party. The rumor eventually spread to staff, and although no one really believed it, friends began avoiding him. As Phil began feeling isolated because of being ignored by his peers, he became bitter.

Harry was astute enough to sense the bitterness Phil was feeling and began relating things he claimed that staff members were saying. "I overheard Officer Jones say he believed the rumors about you. He said that all cooks were radical; otherwise you wouldn't write disciplinaries on staff for snitching a little food now and then. He doesn't realize that you have to report things like that—it's your job. He doesn't know you like we do. If he knew how kind and generous you really are, he wouldn't talk that way. I guess custody treats you cooks just like they treat us inmates. Right?

"You're right," Phil agreed, "if those uniform people

167

would stay the hell out of this kitchen, everyone would be a lot better off."

"By the way, Phil," Harry said, "could I bum another pack of cigarettes from you? My money still hasn't arrived. I'll pay you . . . "

Phil was still mad from hearing about Officer Jones. He handed the cigarettes to Harry without even thinking.

As the rumors gained in force and Black inmates heard about the racially prejudiced cook, a great deal of animosity began building among Black inmates assigned to kitchen duty. One afternoon, a Black inmate cook refused to take an order from Phil, stating that, "No Honkey radicals are going to tell me what to do!"

Phil repeated the order, but this time with the admonition that the offending inmate comply "or get locked up!" The Black inmate assumed a fighting stance and challenged the cook to "get it on" or whatever. The situation became a stand-off. Phil didn't know what to do. He wasn't a fighter. The inmate, on the other hand, was not only a fighter but a weight lifter as well. He glanced around for a custody officer, but there was none. The inmate was blocking the doorway, so there was no way out. Phil began to show his fear. Suddenly, Harry and a friend of his stepped in front of Phil and told the inmate to "back off." They assured the Black man that Phil would take no action, that he would tell no one, and that the whole incident would be forgotten. An agreement was reached with the provision that Phil would give him no further orders. Peace was restored.

Turning to Phil, Harry said, "Where were those goddamned cops when you needed them? That guy could have killed you! You're lucky we were here."

With a great sigh of relief, Phil thanked them and said, "That's one I owe you. I'm sure glad you were here."

Harry's attitude was polite and reassuring when he said,

168

"It looks like those cops don't care about you. One of them is supposed to be in this kitchen all the time. Well, you don't have to worry. As long as I'm around, no Black man is going to harm you."

"You know," Phil said, "I'm going to assign you guys to jobs back here. You won't have to mop any more floors. If you are back here where I work, I won't have to worry about that guy."

"You're O.K. By the way," Harry said, "I don't want to leave. Emotions are still a little hot. Have you any more cigarrettes?"

Phil gave Harry several packages. "You got these coming, and more," he said as he reached for a handshake.

In the days that followed, Phil noticed that each time he entered the vegetable room, the inmates would stop working and stare at him. They would hold their trimming knives across their chests and all conversations ceased. This odd behavior worried him. He decided to share his uneasy feeling with Harry, and he did so.

"That's interesting," said Harry. "Tell you what; tomorrow when you go into the vegetable room, I'll go with you and we'll put a stop to this nonsense."

The next morning, Phil noticed Harry talking to Black inmates. Although he couldn't hear their conversations, he thought it was odd for a person who was extremely prejudiced to be in such close association with them. "Maybe," he thought, "Harry is trying to find out the reason for the behavior in the vegetable room." The thought comforted him. It was time to make the rounds and inspect each kitchen area for cleanliness. The vegetable room was first on the list, but he decided to wait for Harry to finish talking. When Harry finally joined him, Phil asked, "What did you find out?"

"Later, Man." There was an odd commanding tone to Harry's voice. Phil had the feeling that he was being told to shut up. They stepped inside the vegetable room. All work stopped. The knives went to "port arms." No one smiled or spoke. Phil heard that door slam. He looked around for Harry and discovered that it was he who had slammed the door. The look in Harry's eyes was frightening. Fear began to overtake Phil.

"What's going on here?" he demanded.

The vegetable room work crew had now encircled him. They were brandishing their knives in a threatening manner, and they were closing in. On Harry's command, the group stopped. Harry was smiling. He said, "We're friends, ain't we, Phil? . . . "

Phil said nothing.

"Friends do favors for other friends, don't they?"

Still no reply.

"We need a favor, Phil. And you would save us a lot of time, trouble, and nastiness if you just granted it. All we want to do is have a party. We need some way to release our tensions. Oh, we could riot, but people get hurt in riots. We don't want to hurt anyone, so you could do us a favor, the institution a favor, and staff a favor. You can prevent a riot. You'll be a hero. Now, what do you say?"

"How?" There was an uneasy distrust to Phil's voice.

"It's easy," Harry said. "You can't have a party without booze. All you have to do is bring two large bottles in your coat when you come to work tomorrow. No one will ever know. We'll never ask you again, and you will have prevented a riot—saved somebody's life even."

"I can't do that, I'll lose my job!" Phil had difficulty controlling the tremble in his voice.

"Listen, you little bastard!" Harry was yelling. "You don't know the trouble you're in! You think we're playing games? You're in trouble already. You'll do as you are told or these people will kill you! And if you're thinking you'll

170

leave here and report us, I'll have your job! Everyone here is a witness to the radical material you've been bringing in, and I've got all these contraband cigarettes in my cell. Plus the fact that we have friends on the streets that will snuff you in a hot minute!"

Harry paused to let Phil absorb what he had just said; then in a softer voice, he continued. "Now bring the stuff in tomorrow. Place it behind this storage bin and you'll have no further problems with us. Let him go!" Harry commanded.

That evening at home, Phil was quiet, sullen, deep in thought, and when he did speak to members of his family he "snapped" at them. He refused to tell his wife what was wrong, and when she asked him why he had written a twenty-five dollar check, he told her to mind her own business. He had never spoken to her that way before.

(Author's Note) Phil is trying to decide on a course of action. The point should be stressed that to date he has not committed any major offense. True, he used poor judgment, but reporting the incident would bring everything out in the open. If he exposed his tormentors, he could expect the following:

    A. All responsible inmates would be disciplined.
    B. He would NOT lose his job.
    C. His peers would know by his action that the rumors about him were unfounded.
    D. He would be much wiser, and the likelihood that inmates could dupe him in the future much less.
    E. He would be a much better employee.
    F. He would be made to realize that inmates threaten to have friends harm staff members off ground very frequently, but it almost never happens.
    G. Finally, administrators would interview him because of his poor judgment. When they felt assured that he had profitted from the experiences, they would compliment him for exposing the incident.

The next day, Phil placed the contraband where they had told him. As the day progressed, he kept to himself. He was quiet and obviously worried. In his thoughts, he remembered the inmate promised that no further requests of this nature would be made, but somehow he felt no comfort in the thought. He had a feeling in the pit of his stomach that made him want to vomit.

Harry had not reported to work for three days, and Phil was not about to report him. As a matter of fact, he hoped never to see him again. He wanted to forget that Harry ever existed. But that was not in the plan. Harry showed up that afternoon. This time Harry had a list of things he wanted. He didn't have to insist. Phil knew he was in too deep to refuse.

On the way home, Phil thought, "Where will it all end?"

It ended the next day. Officials had become suspicious of Phil's sudden personality change and his worried expression. They placed him under surveillance and arrested him as he was placing the contraband behind the bin.

CASE HISTORY III

Profile—Staff Member

Subject is a thirty-five year old Correctional Sergeant who has been promoted to Correctional Counselor I. He is of Italian extraction, speaks with a slight accent, and has fourteen years' correctional experience as a custodial officer. He is known to be a firm supervisor who expects the best effort of his men, and he is viewed by both staff and inmates as being fair. He came into the correctional field with a high school education, and attended college after work. He achieved an A.A. Degree, then continued with upper division courses until he graduated with a B.A. Degree in Social Science. He is short, stocky and given to idle conversation. His name is Elder.

Profile—Prison Inmate

Subject is a twenty-three year old inmate, also of Italian extraction, who has been incarcerated for the crime of murder. He is a first termer and has served three years of his sentence. He has a fourth grade education, is learning a trade, and is not viewed as a behavior case by the institution. His build is medium and average in height. He has a limited vocabulary. When given job assignments, he is known to be a hard worker, polite and respectful to staff; he is active in prison sports programming. His name is Jones.

The Set-Up

As a newly appointed correctional counselor, Mr. Elder was assigned an office in a housing wing where 125 inmates were living. In this new role he had the responsibility of making board reports and dealing with inmate problems. His former duties as a custodial sergeant were more regimented than those of a counselor and he had difficulty adjusting to the new routine. He was too "hard" they said, and other counselors encouraged him to become more understanding with inmates.

As a sergeant, his function was easy because he understood control techniques. He interpreted the request of his peers to be more understanding as meaning that counselors should not control inmate actions, so he began pretending not to notice minor rule violations. "Besides," he told himself, "enforcing rules is a custody function."

As mentioned earlier in this presentation, inmates in the prison community categorize employees: Some are hard, some are soft and some are mellow. Hard employees go strictly by the "book." Soft employees allow people to walk on them, but mellow employees are people who have put it all together. They know exactly when to use each approach. Some employees can never achieve this middle ground. They are either hard or soft, but they can't be both. Mr. Elder was one such person. In custody, he was hard. As a counselor, he had become soft. Inmates began to notice his inability to adjust to this new job, and began testing him.

Inmate Jones approached Mr. Elder one day and asked if he could mop and wax his floors each evening. "I'm the type of inmate," he said, "who likes to keep busy. It makes time go faster."

"But," Mr. Elder said, "You already have a job."

"I'm finished each day around noon," responded the inmate, "and there's nothing to do but loaf, and I've got too much energy for that. Besides, I like to do things for people. It would be a favor to me if you would accept my offer."

"O.K.," Elder said enthusiastically. "You asked for it, you got it."

Jones was an excellent worker. He waxed and polished and always maintained a pleasant attitude. Elder really liked him. The two men formed a mutual respect for one another and each evening after work they would engage in long conversations. They talked about everything—current events,

174

wars, personal problems, and even their girl friends.

One evening during a lull in the conversation, Jones indicated that he was out of cigarettes. Elder promptly shared his. After all, it was the least he could do in return for everything Jones had done for him. Soon, borrowing cigarettes became a habit. Jones said, "It embarrasses me to be out of smokes so much," but Elder convinced him it was O.K. "You ought to just give me a whole package, then I wouldn't be asking so often," Jones said jokingly.

"Hell, why not?" and Elder gave him the package. The giving of one package led to another and, before long, Jones had twenty packages of cigarettes in his room.

Jones suddenly stopped reporting for work. Thinking something was wrong, Elder went to his room. The two men had been on a first name basis for a long time now. They shared several things in common, and it wasn't in keeping with Jones' life style not showing for work.

Arriving at the room, Elder asked, "What's the matter there, big fellow? It's not like you to sit around doing nothing."

Jones was lying on the bed, staring at the wall. He gave no indication of even hearing Elder. He seemed sad, like the weight of the world was upon him.

Elder tried again, "Hey, friend, it's me, your counselor."

"Oh, hello, Mr. Elder. I'm sorry, I didn't hear you."

"Mr. Elder! What's all this mister stuff? You haven't been down to see me. I just came by to find out why."

Jones' eyes had never left the wall, nor had he altered his position on the bed. Something was wrong all right—bad wrong!

"I want you down in my office at 3:00 p.m. . . . you're on my caseload and you need help. That's what a counselor is for. Be there! That's an order!"

"You've got problems of your own, Mr. Elder. You don't

need the addition of mine."

"That's an order!" again said Elder. Jones was reluctant, but finally agreed.

In the office, Elder sat poised to listen. It was an effort for Jones to talk. He kept groping for words, then finally lost his composure. It had been a long time since Elder had seen tears in a man's eyes. He wasn't sure of how to handle a situation like this, but finally said, "There's no problem that can't be solved. If you will just tell me what is troubling you, perhaps I can help."

After a long silence, Jones stated, "My mother passed away."

"I'm very sorry," Elder said in a consoling tone. "When did it happen?"

"Three days ago." Jones paused, then continued. "I didn't even get to show her how much I've changed. She would have been proud of me."

Elder felt a lump well up in his throat.

"It seems, when one bad problem develops another follows close behind." As Jones spoke he went to the window. Gazing into the sky, he finished his story! "Mom didn't know that I'm in jail. I gave her a fictitious address and told her that I had a job in this city. Friends are putting my young sister on a plane. She'll be here tomorrow. There is no one to care for her now, and she is expecting to live with me. I have no place for her to stay, no money to pay rent even if she did have a place to live. There isn't even anyone to pick her up at the airport. I just don't know what I'm going to do."

For a while there was no conversation at all. The two men seemed deep in thought. Finally, Elder spoke. "Look," he said, "I can pick her up at the airport, and she can stay at my place for a couple of days. Maybe between now and then we can work out a better solution."

Jones gave a long, deep sigh of relief. It was obvious that

a burden had been lifted from him. He smiled for the first time that day. "You don't know what a help you've been, Mr. Elder. I can't thank you enough. If I can ever do anything for you. . . ."

Elder interrupted, "Well, one thing you can do is keep this under your hat. I'm not supposed to board relatives of inmates."

"Man, you can count on me. I won't say a word." Jones' obvious relief was reassuring. Elder felt comfortable, yet a little uneasy with his decision to help.

The girl introduced herself as Shirley. She was very pretty, about eighteen years old, and had a very nice personality. Elder was surprised. He had expected someone much younger. Oh well, not much could be done about it now. He picked up her bags and walked toward the car. On the way home, he couldn't help but notice that she seemed much older than her years. "Experienced" was the word that kept coming into his mind. He assuaged his conscience by concluding that some people are just precocious.

He gave her a tour of the house and she liked it, but indicated that it needed a woman's touch. Elder apologized for leaving her alone, but said he had to return to work and said he'd check with the neighbors when he returned that evening to find her a place to stay. When she was alone, Shirley occupied her time by cleaning the house, and by the time Elder returned each room was a showcase of cleanliness. She also had prepared a sumptuous meal, and while the two of them washed dishes, Shirley told Elder about her religious conversion. Elder liked her and found himself thinking he would hate to see her leave. Because of dinner, their conversation, and doing dishes together, Elder hadn't noticed the time. It was now too late to call the neighbors, so Shirley had to stay in the guest room. Elder assured Shirley he would find her a place to stay right after the weekend. Over the next two days

177

there were many opportunities to talk, but Shirley kept busy and much of the conversation was in between jobs. She made herself invaluable. She cooked, washed clothes and constantly cleaned things.

By all appearances, Monday was going to be just a routine day: Board reports to get out, people to interview, same as any other Monday. Elder supposed he would work until around 3:00 p.m., then go see Inmate Jones and tell him how much he liked his sister. His mind wandered to Shirley, then back to Jones. He could see the family resemblance. He smiled as he thought about kidding Jones for not telling him Shirley was a beautiful woman, not a child as he had been led to believe. "Perhaps," he thought, "Jones doesn't know his sister is a grown woman. After all, he hasn't seen her in three years. She was only fifteen when he went to prison."

Elder decided not to wait. He called Jones to his office. He was anxious to tell him what a wonderful person his sister had turned out to be, and that he would arrange for the two of them to visit. Jones wasn't in his room. The unit officer told Elder that Jones was on a visit—his ex-wife, he thought. Elder decided to meet her. He even considered inviting her over to see Shirley—a sort of family reunion. The idea was pleasing to him. Looking into the visiting room, he saw Jones and Shirley sitting at a table. No one else was there. The officer must have been mistaken when he said ex-wife. "Or," thought Elder, "maybe she would be along later." At any rate, he decided to go in and say hello.

On his way past the visiting room admissions desk, Elder glanced at the guest register. "Inmate's name: Jones; Guest's name: Edna; Relationship: Ex-wife."

Elder couldn't believe what he was reading. He was confused. He knew from reading Jones' file that he (Jones) had been married before; but that was Shirley visiting him. There had to be some mistake.

178

Standing by the table, Elder excused himself and said, "Shirley, I think there's been a mistake . . . "

"There's no mistake," Jones said. "Sit down." His tone was rough and commanding. Elder sat down. Jones continued, "I've got a list of things I want you to buy." He produced the list from his shirt pocket. Shirley, or Edna, or whoever she was, hadn't spoken a word. Her facial expression was cold and calculating. She looked hard and angry.

Elder was tense. His eyes went from Shirley to Jones, then to the list. "Benzedrine, Tenuate, Dexedrin . . . "

"These are drugs! I can't do that!" Elder was becoming excited.

Jones told him to shut up and to keep his voice down. Shirley spoke for the first time since Elder entered the visiting room. "Listen, you dumb bastard. You'll do it, or you won't have a job!" Looking at Jones, she asked, "You still got them cigarettes?"

"Yep, two cartons. Twenty packages, and he brought them in. And another thing," Jones continued, "where do you get off sleeping with my wife?"

Shirley spoke again. "Now listen, you son-of-a-bitch, you get them drugs and you get them today, or I'll tell the Superintendent I'm living with you. . . . "

Elder regained his composure, stood up sharply and interrupted her demand. "Save your breath. I'll tell him myself," and he stormed out of the room.

Elder's report was complete in every detail. Jones was locked up, Edna was removed from the approved visiting list, and the counselor was suspended with pay for fifteen days, pending investigation. He was later reinstated with the admonition that another display of poor judgment would result in a more lasting type of punishment.

179

CASE HISTORY IV

Profile—Staff Member

Subject is a twenty-six year-old divorcee of Hispanic origin. She is the mother of three children, very religious, overly-friendly, very trusting, and deeply compassionate. She has eighteen months' service in corrections and is a vocational secretary. She is tall, slender and considered attractive. Her personality is outgoing, she believes everyone can be a "Born again Christian," regardless of their crimes, and her mission in life is to propagate her religious convictions. Her name is Eva.

Profile—Prison Inmate

Subject is a twenty-five year old male Caucasian who is incarcerated for the crime of murder. He is intelligent, cunning and con-wise. He is a fourth termer who is known to be a manipulator. He is tall, nice looking, and works hard on his job assignments. He is married to a known prostitute. He has no children and openly expresses his hatred for the children of other people. He refuses to learn a trade or complete his education.

The Set-Up

Eva was assigned to the prison vocational shops area as a secretary. Her staff consisted of one inmate clerk. She was able to observe his work habits closely because the two of them were alone for about an hour each day. She noticed he was intelligent, highly efficient and performed his duties in a calm and organized fashion. He was quiet, and other than conversation about work, he said very little. After approximately three months, Eva decided to find out what her inmate clerk knew about God. She began her conversation by saying, "As efficient and capable as you appear to be, you could

180

have been very successful in the free society. What caused you to come to prison?"

"Oh, I guess one reason I turned to crime," he responded, "was that my wife had expensive tastes. She wanted things I couldn't afford. She said she was tired of living from hand-to-mouth and was considering a divorce. We had three children, so in order to keep my family together, I began stealing. I'm sorry I committed the crimes now because she went ahead with the divorce."

Being a highly emotional person, Eva's heart went out to him in deep sorrow over the cruel circumstances that led him to prison. She commiserated, "I'm very sorry, but I know what you're going through. I also suffered a divorce, and like you, I have three children."

They discussed the difficulties faced by lone parents in raising children, and Eva shared how her relationship with God helped her through it all.

"I, too, have had a religious conversion since coming to jail," her clerk told her, "but God isn't helping me much. I had to leave my children with an older woman who has barely enough money to care for herself, and my youngest child is suffering from severe malnutrition—she's very ill."

"What about welfare?" Eva inquired.

"Prisoners can't get welfare," he said, somewhat astonished that Eva was so ill-informed.

The similarities in their circumstances created a closeness, and a friendship born out of empathy was formed. Because he felt that she understood, the clerk kept Eva informed daily of his daughter's steadily worsening condition.

About three weeks later, the inmate failed to report for duty. In an attempt to find out what was wrong, Eva called his unit and ordered him to come to work. It was after staff members had left the vocational office that he finally reported for work. He didn't greet her as he normally did, nor did he look in her direction. Finally Eva decided on a face-to-face confrontation, and discovered the man was crying.

"What in the world is the matter?" she demanded.

After a few moments of trying to regain his composure, the clerk finally confided that his youngest daughter had died of malnutrition, and he broke down again. Eva couldn't contain herself. She tried to console him by putting her arms around him and placing his head on her shoulder. The scenario was highly emotional. The inmate finally backed away, saying, "Don't! If someone saw you doing this, they would never understand, and you could get into trouble."

"To hell with what people think," she said.

"No," he said, "we have to be realistic."

Experiences like this are not easily overcome, so in the days that followed it was necessary for Eva to provide a great deal of consolation.

After a period of time the inmate said, "I probably won't be seeing you after today. My son is ill, and I have no intention of letting him die." He produced a money order for one hundred dollars and continued by saying, "It's illegal to have this, and if I get caught, and there's no doubt in my mind that I will be caught, I'll go to outside court. My time will be extended and I will be moved to another prison. But to save my son, I'll run that risk. It's a value judgment based on right or wrong; and sometimes the law is wrong."

Deeply concerned, the woman considered, "There must be another way."

"Well," he responded, "there's not!"

After about an hour, he said, "There is one other way I could get the money to my children and no one would be caught; but I wouldn't even consider asking."

"Tell me," she said.

"Well, if you really want to know, I've never done this sort of thing, but I knew a guy who did. It's one of those one-time-only things.

"If I were to place this envelope in your purse without your knowing it, and you discovered it when you got home, all you would have to do is sign the money order and mail it. It's not like being dishonest, because you didn't know it was there, so it's not a premeditated act. Your signing the money order would make it appear like a gift from a concerned person who didn't want to see a kid starve, and it couldn't be traced to the institution. But, no way would I ask you to do a thing like that. Besides, it's my problem, not yours. You asked me, so I told you." During the remainder of the day he quoted several passages in the scripture where Christians violated the law to save a brother's life.

During the next few days, very little was said about the money order, but the baby's condition had become critical. The child was expected to die within thirty-six hours. That evening, when Eva arrived home, she opened her purse and discovered the money order. She paced the floor wondering what to do. She prayed for guidance, read God's word in the scripture her clerk had told her about, and finally concluded that the prison law was wrong. What the inmate needed was an act of charity—a small violation of a rule to save a human life. She signed the money order, included a personal check of her own for twenty-five dollars, and a note asking the woman who was caring for the children to keep her advised of the baby's health. In the days that followed, it was obvious that a burden had been lifted from her clerk. The child improved, but the subject of the money order was never again discussed.

One day he began, "You know so much about me, I might as well tell you the real reason my wife divorced me." Hesitating and groping for words, he continued, "I'm not much of a man, because I can't achieve an erection. I'm sorry," he added quickly, "I shouldn't be discussing a thing

183

like this with you, it's too embarrassing."

"No, no, it's all right," she responded, "you need to get it out. We're both mature people. Have you seen a doctor?"

"Many," he answered, "they tell me it's all in my mind. That's nice to know, but how does one overcome such an affliction?"

The new problem permitted deep personal, clinically-based discussion about sexual techniques. As time passed the inmate shared that one doctor indicated that the only thing that would help him was to find some patient, understanding woman. "But," he said, "I never ran into a person like you on the streets."

One day, just as the custody officer had made his rounds, and the inmate knew he wouldn't be back for over two hours, he announced, "I'm going to do something that really isn't right. I hope you will understand, but I've got to know!" With that, he exposed himself. "See that," he exclaimed, "I'm no man at all!"

Eva was shocked! She became hysterical and cried, "Don't do that, you'll get us both in trouble!"

His voice was determined and urgent. "That custodial officer won't be back for a long time, and you don't understand! I've got to know! You are probably the only woman that can make a man out of me. As much as I desire you, nothing is happening. If you would just touch me, I'm sure it would make a difference." He grabbed her hand and pulled it toward his penis.

It was at that precise moment that the custodial officer walked in. For some reason he had reversed his customary pattern and returned to the vocational office. He arrested the inmate, reported the secretary, and she was escorted off grounds.

In the investigation that followed, the inmate stated that he was not guilty. The secretary, he stated, had paid him

184

one hundred dollars for his sexual favors and he could prove it. His wife, a prostitute, came to the institution and presented a sealed envelope with the money order signed by the secretary and bearing her return address. The inmate's wife stated that as a prostitute, she understood the needs of men in confinement, and if this former employee was willing to pay for sex, she had no objections.

Even though the employee included a note indicating genuine concern for the child, the fact she had mailed a letter knowing it was in direct violation of institution rules, and that she was discovered in a compromising situation with a prisoner, was sufficient provocation to terminate her employment.

CASE HISTORY V

Profile—Staff Member

Subject is a thirty-five year old male Caucasian who works in a women's prison as a maintenance man. He is six feet tall, weighs approximately 195 lbs. and has blond hair and blue eyes. He is married, has two children, is active in community affairs and is considered a capable employee. He has been a correctional employee for approximately two years and has an excellent performance record. His temperament is mild, and he enjoys the love and respect of his family. His name is Jack.

Profile—Inmate:

Subject is a twenty-three year old Caucasian who has been incarcerated for the crime of murder. She is a drug addict who supported her habit as a prostitute. She has been married three times but there is no record of her having divorced any of these men. She has an extensive arrest record, and prognosis for rehabilitation is poor. She is blond, small in stature—5 ft. 3 in., has blue eyes and weighs approximately 105 lbs. In the institution setting she is known to be a gang leader. Her intelligence is high normal.

The Set-Up

At a women's prison facility on the West Coast several maintenance men gathered near their office each morning to discuss the day's activities. As prisoners passed this area going to job assignments, the men took pleasure in observing their movements and on occasions cast sexual aspersions loud enough for the women to hear. Women in confinement appreciate male attention because it provides a diversion from their normal routine. To assure its continuance, some of them would make adjustments in wearing apparel exposing

186

portions of their under garments. Particularly taken by these impromptu displays was a man named Jack who gave these ladies the impression of mentally disrobing them. Toni, a small attractive blond inmate, seemed to excite Jack more than the others, so she took special pains providing him with a good show. Her acting, superb and polished, was designed to show embarrassment at being discovered, but not to an extent which might discourage Jack.

Toni decided to apply for the job of maintenance orderly. She arranged with the incumbent to resign, and extracted a promise from inmate yard leaders that no other prisoner would apply for the position. As there were no other applicants, she was hired immediately.

Everyone in maintenance was impressed with Toni's efficiency. She was polite, indefatigable and exceptionally well-versed on office procedure. Her demeanor was above reproach, except for occasions where she found herself alone in the office with Jack, whereupon situations involving clothing adjustments continued to occur. The ensuing weeks found Toni and Jack becoming quite friendly. They had many personal discussions. They shared many of the same interests and Toni let Jack know she liked him very much. He was different, she told him. His attitude and the way he approached inmates made them feel they were people, not just numbers. "As for myself," she said, "when you're around I'm somebody. There's something about you that makes me feel I'm all woman. You make me feel good about life, and that's a feat many have tried but could never accomplish. If I had known someone like you on the 'streets'," she continued, "I never would have been in jail."

As time passed Toni's personality changed. She seemed in a state of depression much of the time. Her normal friendly attitude had become cool and indifferent. Jack was concerned and indicated he'd like to help. She didn't want to burden him with her problems, saying, "you have enough on your hands with a wife and two kids; you don't need the addition of my troubles." However, Jack insisted. Toni sat silently considering Jack's offer. The, bursting into tears, she said: "for well over a week now, two girls in my unit have been pressuring me for sex. I've been able to handle them up to now, but last night they had a knife and threatened to kill me if I don't cooperate. I don't want to do it, but I may have no choice. It's been so long since I've been with a man I'm afraid I might enjoy their attention. I've been trying to save myself for someone like you. I don't know how much longer I can hold out. I'm so frightened I don't know what to do!"

She began sobbing uncontrollably. Jack's heart went out to her. "You poor kid!" he said, placing his arms around her. Toni's hand "unwittingly" fell to Jack's groin. Embracing for a long moment they stood silently looking into each other's eyes. The sound of someone approaching broke the spell. Both tried to appear busy, but the message was clear. Each knew the other's thoughts, each knew what would have happened if it had not been for their intruder.

Even though he avoided the office for the next few days, Jack couldn't get Toni and the excitement of her actions off his mind. He knew the rules, but justified his desire by convincing himself that he wouldn't go all the way, just play around, who'd ever know?

Later in the day Jack returned to the office thinking he would apologize to Toni and hope he hadn't left her with any false impressions. As he spoke, Toni crossed her legs exposing her thighs, then stood and walked into the storage room— Jack followed.

Storage room excursions were by now a common occurrence. Jack had thrown caution to the winds and assuaged his conscience with the notion that no normal man could withstand exposure to Toni's tempting body. If discovered he was sure his boss would understand.

Several days later Toni went into the storage room and as usual Jack followed. But this time Toni rejected his advances. She looked worried. Confused, Jack said, "what's wrong with you?" "I'm pregnant," she said without hesitation, "and it's your kid!" Her voice gave no space for denial, and her stoic expression was hard. An indescribable panic surged through every vein in Jack's body, as Toni shouted, "DRUGS! I need drugs, and, you're going to get them!" She spoke in command tones removing any thought Jack may have had about negotiation. With the confidence and outreach of a seasoned drill sergeant she said, "Did you hear me, stupid? Tomorrow morning, at this time, in this room, I want marijuana—two kilo's (approximately 4 lbs.). No excuses. Don't bring it and I go straight to The Man!"

The reality of the situation began dawning on Jack. He said, "I can't do that! I've never bought dope in my life! I wouldn't know where to start looking!"

"That's your problem, sucker. You knew what you were getting into. Get smart, honey!" The soft, sweet, helpless little girl of a moment ago, had suddenly become cold, hard, and ruthless. The transition made Jack's head swim. The word "helpless" froze in his mind. "Helpless," he thought. "That's it! Toni!" he shouted, "you're helpless! Those women pressuring you! You can't help what you're doing. They made you do this!" Jack's revelation made her laugh.

"How stupid can you be! I've seen some squares, but, buddy, you take the cake! Nobody pressures me in this joint, I pressure them!" Toni started to leave, then almost as if it were an afterthought, she turned and said, "Remember, tomorrow, this time, this place, no excuses."

Being ignorant of street-buying techniques, Jack was unable to make the purchase. He feared going to work the next day, but at the same time he knew he had to show. He just needed more time.

While waiting for everyone to leave the office, Jack wondered what he would say to Toni. Would she give him more time, or would she report him? Sensing that Toni was looking at him, his eyes went in her direction. She was smiling. Not with arrogance as he expected, but with friendliness. It was the same sweet smile of an earlier time, and seemed to be offered with an attitude of understanding. Passing his desk on the way to the storage room she said, "Come on, baby, I have something for you." Confused by Toni's unexpected behavior, Jack followed. He started to explain and Toni quickly touched his lips with her fingers. "Shh," she said softly, "not till we've loved each other."

Later, with the impish sweetness of a little girl, she said, "I'm sorry. I was wrong speaking so harshly to you yesterday. Forgive me?"

There was a sincerity in her voice that was making Jack feel maybe she wasn't all bad; that perhaps she did have his best interest at heart. Yet, there was something about her niceness Jack could only sense. A cautious feeling like men have after accidentally firing a rifle; you know the weapon is safe but only if you follow the safety rules. "I wonder what the safety rules are going to be?"

Toni continued, "After you went home I realized you had no way of knowing how to buy that much grass, you've been a square all your life. Here's the address of a man to call. He'll supply the stuff. All you have to do is pay for it and bring it in."

The world Jack thought he might be able to rebuild had just crumbled again. She hadn't changed, she was simply using a different approach. "What if I refuse?" Jack said, still thinking he might be able to escape the inevitable.

"You have a good job, a good reputation, a wife and two kids. Refuse and tomorrow you'll have absolutely nothing." Though her voice remained calm, her eyes told the story. There was no way out. Touching his face lightly, Toni smiled and continued, " Cheer up, honey, it's not the end of the world. It is the world. It's what's happening out there. And there's no reason you and I can't continue using this storeroom for our own pleasure—you be good to me and I'll be good to you—O.K.?" She turned and left the room.

After several months, Toni's pregnancy could no longer be concealed. When questioned she freely named Jack as the father. Jack could have denied the charge but he didn't. He was tired. Tired of lying to his wife about the money he was spending for marijuana. Tired of associating with criminals. Tired of the constant guilt gnawing inside him. Tired of worry and the inescapable fear of being caught. But most of all he was tired of Toni. He confessed.

(Authors' note:) Toni knew that Jack would not know how to make a marijuana contact. She waited until the next day to let the gravity of the situation sink in before supplying him with the marijuana contact's name. She had to assure herself that he would not go to authorities even with the powerful lever she had hanging over him.

CASE HISTORY VI

Profile—Widow

Subject is a sixty-five year-old female Caucasian who was recently widowed. She is a woman of average means who enjoys keeping her small home and garden looking nice, and she is respected in the neighborhood as a community-minded citizen. She is tall, slender and considered attractive for her age. Her personality is outgoing and friendly. Her husband's death provided her with a lump sum insurance premium, the amount of which she freely discusses with friends. She has been extremely lonely since the passing of her spouse.

Profile—Bunco Artists

Subjects comprise a two-man bunco team who extort life savings from women living alone. They are intelligent, articulate, and sensitive to moods, statements, and body language of their victims. Their friendly nature, confidence, handsome features and ability to project themselves as honest, concerned citizens, opens many doors. Their partnership is a June-September age arrangement with the older of the two being the Turner in this case.

The Set-Up

Mrs. Miltown was overheard discussing her $44,000 insurance settlement from her husband's death with a friend in the grocery store. "I just don't know what to do with so much money. I've never had to deal with finances. Before, my husband always took care of that aspect of our life. Anyway, I've put it all in the bank for safekeeping until I decide what to do with it."

Two men, Mr. Powers and Mr. York, who had been eavesdropping on the conversation decided to try to cash in on the money (selection of a victim). They found out where she lived, established a "stake out" to learn her patterns of behavior and discovered she worked in her flower garden around 10:00 a.m. each morning (the observation process). Mr. Powers passed her home each day and soon formed the habit of commenting on the health and beauty of her plants. The two people became "over-the-fence" friends. Powers designed his comments and questions to discover Mrs. Miltown's likes and dislikes (the testing process) which turned out to be amazingly similar to his own. He praised her ideas and indicated complete agreement with her beliefs and disbeliefs (the support system).

During one of their morning conversations, Mrs. Miltown inquired into the nature of Mr. Powers' profession. Displaying a badge, Powers explained his duties as a plain-clothes policeman was to protect people in the neighborhood. This new assignment came about because of increased crime in the area with criminals concentrating on women without husbands. Mrs. Miltown shared the recent loss of her husband and indicated that knowing Powers was on the job gave her a sense of security. Finding his emotions difficult to control, Powers told of the recent passing away of his wife. In an effort to console him, Mrs. Miltown invited Powers in for coffee (empathy/sympathy). They discussed the problem of being alone and how couples with marriages still intact no longer included them in social affairs. A great deal of time was spent nurturing feelings of bitterness the two were acquiring because former friends had excluded them (the we/they syndrome), but they found solace in their newly discovered friendship. Powers indicated his sanity was predicated on their future association (plea for help). Mr. Powers became Tom to her, and Mrs. Miltown, whom he now called Mildred, assured him her home was his home.

Without explanation several days passed in which Tom made no contact with Mildred. She had come to rely on the visits and experienced extreme loneliness and worry. Finally, Tom returned. Mildred's exuberant embrace and Tom's reciprocal hug indicated feelings deeper than mere friendship (the touch system).

After a while, Tom explained his absence saying he was investigating a criminal plot to extort funds from women in the community, and that he had discovered Mildred was one of the gang's intended victims. Mildred was shocked and fearful, but Tom assured her he had a plan to catch the culprits and she need not worry (offer of protection).

He told her the gang's method of operation was to gain a sample of their intended victim's handwriting, forge a bank passbook and withdraw the person's savings. "However," he said, "we discovered in your case the gang is in possession of information that, if exposed, would incriminate you!"

Mildred was confused. "Incriminate me, but I haven't done anything wrong!" she shouted.

"Now calm down and hear me out." Tom's voice was soothing and unexcited as he continued. "They have discovered that your late husband misrepresented the exact amount of his earnings to the Internal Revenue Service. I checked it out and he did. If the passbook ruse fails—you know, the clerk becomes suspicious—they plan to get out of the bank quickly, wait a few days, contact you by phone and threaten to expose the tax fraud (the lever) unless you give them the money." Mildred began crying. Tom placed his arms around her saying, "They apparently are astute enough about tax law to know that because you signed the form, you're responsible for the acts of your husband and could possibly be jailed. But I have a plan to keep this from happening."

Sobbing almost uncontrollably, Mildred managed to say, "I remember situations where monies were eliminated from the tax form, but my husband assured me the omission violated no laws."

Hugging her tightly, Tom said, "Hey, I'm on your side! I know you're honest, and if you cooperate with me, I'll have these guys behind bars before they can use their information, and it will just be our secret" (another offer of protection). Her composure somewhat regained, Mildred assured Tom she would cooperate in any way she could. "That's great, honey." The expression just slipped out.

Tom apologized, but Mildred was pleased. "No apologies necessary," she said. "I'm glad you feel free to express yourself."

The following day, Tom took Mildred to the bank and introduced her to a dignified, well-dressed man who appeared to be moving around the busy desks surveying his domain. "This is Mr. York," Tom said. "I've told him all about my plan and he has agreed to work with the law to apprehend these extortionists. I'll let him explain what we're going to do."

York motioned for Mrs. Miltown to follow him out of the bank. While crossing the street, he explained he had taken an office where he and a few standby policemen could observe and be on hand in the event something went wrong. Once inside he displayed credentials indicating he was actually the bank examiner. "We're grateful you're willing to assist us, Mrs. Miltown. It's because of people like you and Tom here, that this country is safe to live in." York seated Tom and Mildred as he continued to outline the plan. "Secrecy," he admonished, "is absolutely essential." After a brief pause to assure himself Mildred understood, he went on. "According to what Tom tells me, the extortion gang will send one man into the bank with the forged passbook. Tom will be inside watching. He has no way of knowing who the criminal is unless something unusual takes place to arouse his suspicion. For security reasons, none of our tellers have been informed this gang is operating in the area, so one of them might mistakenly give out your money. At all cost, we must guard against that happening. So this is where you come in, Mildred. You go over and withdraw your money, then bring it to me for safekeeping (shopping list). When the gang member attempts to withdraw funds from a closed account, the teller will become suspicious and signal security, at which time Tom will arrest the man inside and the officers with me will apprehend the men outside. Well," York, said, "what do you think of the plan, Mildred?"

She was elated. "An excellent plan!" She complimented them several times, then indicated she was eager to get started.

In what was obviously a tone of gratitude, together with an expression of admiration, Tom touched Mildred's hand, wished the project success, and asked if he could have the privilege of escorting her to dinner when the gang was safely behind bars. The tenderness of the moment caused Mildred to envision a deeper future relationship between the two of them, and she accepted the invitation.

Mildred withdrew the money and gave it to Mr. York. He thanked her again, then suggested she wait for Tom at her home because several days may pass before the bunco artists make their move. "But," he assured her, "I will redeposit your money as soon as Tom makes the arrests." She never saw Powers or York again (the sting).

Profile
of
Susceptibility
Traits and
Statistics

When a pilot is guiding an airplane down the runway on take-off, the aircraft will eventually reach a point of no return. The pilot is committed. He must get the plane into the air. If something goes wrong at this point, there is not enough existing runway to stop, so he either becomes airborne or crashes. The same is true of a set-up. It, too, has a point of no return, and once that point has been reached, there is no turning back; both staff and inmate are committed. Both parties are guilty of rule infractions and neither wishes to be exposed.

What kind of people reach this point of no return, and what happens to them? The authors have researched 106 cases, interviewed numerous employees and friends of employees who were victimized, and sought information from institution investigators. The information contained in this segment of the study was obtained from five prisons in the

United States. The cases were selected at random and involved 133 employees and 112 inmates. The number of inmates does not reflect the total number of team members, contacts, runners, or pointmen; it only covers the ones on record in the reports.

TABLE I				
	Caucasian	Black	Hispanic	Other	Total
Male	24½%	19½%	15%	2%	61%
Female	13½%	12½%	13%	0%	39%
Total	38%	32%	28%	2%	100%

Per cent of Employees by Ethnic and Sex (133 Employees)

	Caucasian	Black	Hispanic	Other	Total
Male	22%	25%	13%	3%	63%
Female	14%	12%	11%	0%	37%
Total	36%	37%	24%	3%	100%

Per cent of Custody by Ethnic and Sex (76 Employees or 57%)

	Caucasian	Black	Hispanic	Other	Total
Male	28%	12%	18%	0%	58%
Female	12%	14%	18%	0%	42%
Total	40%	26%	36%	0%	100%

Per cent of Non-custody by
Ethnic and Sex (57 Employees or 43%)

When compared to the total number of staff members employed by the five institutions, the authors could find no classification that would identify one group of employees as being more susceptible to a set-up than another group (See Table I). Neither ethnic group, sex, nor job assignment helped or hindered an employee's resistance to coercion or threat.

The length of service in corrections (from hiring to time of the researched employees' investigation) was considered. This pointed to an area of susceptibility (See Table II).

TABLE II			
Length òf Service	Custody	Non-Custody	Total
1-11 months	67%	59%	63%
1-3 years	23%	19%	21%
3-8 years	6%	15%	10½%
8-16 years	4%	7%	5½%
	Length of service (133 Employees)		

New employees are hit the hardest. Perhaps this occurs because of the transition lag from free society values and expectations to the confined society values and expectations. Inmates try to coerce new employees before staff-encouraged professionalism is established or before the procedures, rules, and convict communication code are known by the staff member. Unfortunately, inmates sometimes win.

Although experience is no real protector, the chances of victim selection (See Accidental Selection section) are greatly reduced after the first year of employment and again after the third. And although sixteen percent of compromised employees had served in corrections over three years, most

199

employees appear to have learned how to cope after this period.

What kind of levers were acquired on the employees in the study? As a group, forty-nine percent brought in marijuana or pills; eleven percent brought in alcohol; fourteen percent brought in cigarettes; eleven percent brought in clothing, food, or other small items; four percent brought in money; and two percent brought in pornographic material. On others, the acquired levers were eleven percent (female) the granting of sexual favors (and then marijuana or pills); and one percent (male) succumbing to homosexual pressure. Some employees, eight percent, were suspected of bringing in marijuana or pills. (This totals up to 111 percent because the females granting sexual favors later brought in marijuana or pills.)

The type of delivered contraband or granted favors seemed to influence the disposition of a particular case. Sixty-five percent of the staff members granted contraband or favors that were severe enough to terminate their employment—either by firing or forced resignation. Those who brought in smaller items were temporarily suspended, but they did not lose their jobs. No official disposition was recorded for the rest of the employees because either the evidence was insufficient, or the employees, themselves, reported the incident. (See Table III).

Firing prison or jail staff members is a costly business. Investigators are spending more time delving into illegal contraband cases than ever before. In addition, all employees' paid wages, training expenditures, vested time, experience, and years of service, are lost forever. This same loss is true when institutional personnel resign. People who resign from the correctional profession never state inmate pressure as their reason for leaving. However, it has been estimated that between thirty to forty percent of them terminate their em-

200

ployment rather than have their supervisors and peers discover they have been victimized by inmates.

Inmates know that they will fare much better in the disposition of their cases than the staff members. They use personnel to deliver part of their backlash. When a set-up is exposed, the inmates may have lost their investment of time and effort, but it is obvious that staff victims of a set-up are dealt with more harshly than their manipulators. Staff involvement resulted in punitive action for most; whereas, inmate involvement hardly caused any reprimand at all. Table IV elucidates.

TABLE III

Percent in group	Contraband or Favors
59%	marijuana or pills
17%	alcohol
6%	money
1%	homosexual favors (male)
17%	sexual favors (female) and then marijuana or pills

Employment terminated
(87 staff members or 65%)

63%	cigarettes
29%	pornographic material
8%	food, clothing, small items

Employment suspended
(24 staff members or 18%)

100%	suspected of bringing in marijuana or pills

No action: Insufficient evidence
(11 staff members or 8½%)

36%	food items
27%	cigarettes
27%	books or writing materials
10%	T-shirts

No action: Employees reported
themselves (11 staff members or 8½%)

DISPOSITION OF CASES   (133 Employees)

TABLE IV

Disposition for Employees	Disposition for Inmates
65% were expelled or resigned under pressure	64% received no disciplinary action because they cooperated with investigators.
18% were suspended.	12% received ten days isolation: suspended.
8% received no disciplinary action due to insufficient evidence.	16% received ten days isolation.
8% reported themselves; No action taken.	8% were transferred.

CASE DISPOSITIONS

Employee Susceptibility Traits: A Self Test

~~~~~~

The following is a composite of traits that reoccurred in all or part of the 133 employees sampled. The underlying philosophy of each victim in the study was, "Why make a guy's life more difficult than it already is?" Many of the traits listed below are appropriate—even demanded in the free society, but must be treated with care in the confined society. It appears that it is up to the individual to quickly learn the rules of a prison community.

If you, the reader, would like to know your own susceptibility traits, check the ones that apply to you in the free society. In the confined society, these traits are sought by inmates, so self-awareness would help enable you to monitor your own responses.

Are you:

- ☐ easily befriended?
- ☐ overly friendly or overly-familiar with most people?
- ☐ naive to intentions or hidden messages?
- ☐ gullible to stories?
- ☐ susceptible to the you/me syndrome?
- ☐ so sympathetic to others' problems that rules seem secondary?
- ☐ usually timid?

Do you:

- ☐ not know how to handle compliments in a business-like manner?
- ☐ share personal problems?
- ☐ have a trusting nature?
- ☐ believe what you are told without checking on the validity of the information?
- ☐ have a desire to help the underdog?
- ☐ return favor for favor?
- ☐ have difficulty taking command or control?
- ☐ ignore slightly personal or embarrassing remarks and forget instead of directly and immediately addressing them?
- ☐ have difficulty saying NO?
- ☐ circumvent minor rules?

Can you:

- ☐ be made to feel obligated?
- ☐ be made to look the other way and pretend not to notice if the rule being violated is "no big thing?"

If you were a prison employee, would you:

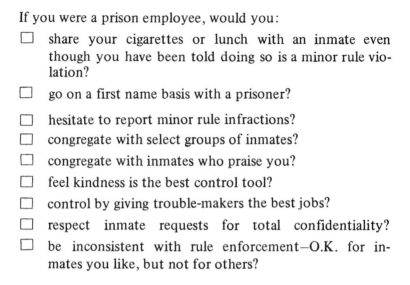

- ☐ share your cigarettes or lunch with an inmate even though you have been told doing so is a minor rule violation?
- ☐ go on a first name basis with a prisoner?
- ☐ hesitate to report minor rule infractions?
- ☐ congregate with select groups of inmates?
- ☐ congregate with inmates who praise you?
- ☐ feel kindness is the best control tool?
- ☐ control by giving trouble-makers the best jobs?
- ☐ respect inmate requests for total confidentiality?
- ☐ be inconsistent with rule enforcement—O.K. for inmates you like, but not for others?

Interestingly, some of the traits inmates look for in trying to find a person susceptible to a set-up are the same traits corrections look for when hiring their employees. Correctional systems want their employees to be kind, have a trusting nature (as opposed to a suspicious one), be empathic and sympathic, have a desire to help the underdog, etc. Prison administrators view these traits as strengths, whereas, under given conditions, inmates see them as weaknesses. If you answered in the affirmative to many of the traits, it does not mean you are unsuited for correctional employment. It does not mean you should change your approach in the free society. It does mean that you would have to proceed with caution and, in some cases, find an alternative approach in your dealings with inmates.

You Can
Feel
IT
in the
Air

~~~~~~

Games Criminals Play presents a subject one rarely discusses in polite society because the process deals with an aspect of human interaction that can be embarrassing and sometimes harmful. The subject has been largely ignored in many circles in the hopes that inattention would cause its disappearance, but it has not gone away and, since unsuspecting honest people as well as the perpetrators suffer from this malady, it must be addressed. Set-ups are one of society's cancers that when properly treated can be easily cured, but to effect a remedy, one must understand how and which medication to apply. Great care must be taken in treatment because the disease is communicable. Both germ carrier and germ receiver must be considered in equal measure, with staff initiating the prevention or treatment measures.

Prison authorities have long been aware of the ability prisoners possess for modifying the behavior of inmate keep-

207

ers, but they have been helpless in combating the process because until now no tool for early recognition has existed. Most people who enter the field of corrections are tested by inmate manipulators. When team members determine it would be difficult to cause that particular honest person to commit a dishonest act, they leave him or her alone and go in search of someone else. The procedure is on-going and constant. In the past when the more experienced employees have stopped or prevented a set-up, there was no patterned input to substantiate that a set-up was in fact going on. Their suspicion was based strictly on feelings, an inner awareness that made them uneasy, and that they themselves did not fully understand. This ability to sense something has gone awry is an extremely important issue and because of the importance to control and treat prisoners, the reader should take a moment to explore the "why" of this trait.

That "Gut Level Feeling"

The manipulation of staff behavior by prison inmates is difficult to explore because most often the suspicion of something being wrong has no initial foundation in fact, but is simply something one feels. There is an innate desire in human beings to want good to come from their relationships with others, so when this inner feeling of uneasiness occurs, there is a tendency of people to chide themselves and cast the matter aside as foolish. Except in special cases, they rarely analyze the feeling. This is because most people tend to fear or back away from situations or feelings they find difficult to comprehend. However, in corrections, feelings are an aspect of the business that should never be ignored or set aside without strong analysis.

Responding to one's feelings is an area everyone in corrections should explore. At one time or another in their lives, most people have had the surprising and sometimes awesome experience of "knowing" in advance of a situation that is going to occur. When this happens, the person may become uneasy with the event because the experience bears an aura of mysticism. Venturing into the unknown is uncomfortable for most people because it means loss of control. As time passes and they relate the experience to friends, they do it in a manner showing pleasure over their ability to predict the future. Yet they are not willing to perfect the trait because most of them fear things they cannot understand. Even though they avoid analyzing this inner awareness, the experience still occurs from time to time. Everyone is endowed with an extrasensory perceptibility which could be used in much greater depth were it not for the fear of being wrong. But people tend to shy away from signs based on feelings.

Corrections is an esoteric profession where a percentage of people develop their inner awareness because of its safety advantage. By not fearing the unknown, these sensitive people analyze their feelings and do not ignore them. Feelings are sometimes the only clue that problems are developing. Over the years many labels have been attached to this phenomenon: extrasensory perception, intuition, inner awareness, suspicion, and the gut level feeling or "feeling it in the air" are but a few. Regardless of the title, people who experience this profound inner knowing will attest to its value and validity.

Most situations occurring in prisons where people respond to their inner feelings almost always produce positive results. However, a caution is in order at this point. There is a difference between fleeting thoughts of danger that quickly pass and lingering feelings of inner awareness. The fleeting suspicion shared with indiscretion can earn one the reputation of being paranoid, but the lingering inner feeling, when sensibly discussed with one's peers or supervisor, can be a harbinger for safety.

Some time has been spent on the concept of inner awareness as a sensing mechanism for one very important reason. In every set-up case researched, the victim became uneasy over the unusual attention being received, and the feeling generated during the early stages of the manipulation process. All victims managed to convince themselves of wrongfully interpreting actions and information. If a powerful lever had been acquired, it was too late to help them or their deceptors.

Games Criminals Play offers guidelines for determining a person's true intentions. It suggests methods of separating behavior sincerely directed toward honesty and self-betterment from actions perpetrated for dishonest gain. This text not only identifies the problem and shows how to prevent it from occurring, but its application generates the re-establishment of relationships between manipulator and victim in a fashion that permits respect between its principals. It is a treatment tool which is designed to discover inappropriate behavior in the early stages and prevent it from continuing. Thus, punitive action never becomes necessary for staff or inmates.

Training Benefits

The advent and implementation of set-up prevention training has produced some amazing, unpredicted results. Three are most notable: (1) improved staff confidence and professionalism, (2) greater receptiveness by inmates to the treatment programs: and (3) better staff/inmate relations. People who travel in unfamiliar territory without using a map run the risk of being lost. They panic and often display inappropriate behavior. Prison employees who discover they are in the throes of manipulation often react in this same manner. *Games Criminals Play* is a map which makes set-up behavior familiar to them. By understanding the behavior and its pit-falls, they can deal with both the act and actors. Knowledge brings confidence and this confidence gives the inspiration necessary for professionalism. This feeling spills over into other areas of the job and becomes contagious to others.

Clearing the air and confronting issues before problems develop removes team members' temptation and allows for no wishful thinking. This employee prevention step provides consistency in treatment and control, thus building reciprocal respect with the inmates. Keeper and kept interact on a daily basis in a positive manner benefiting both groups. The authors of this compilation have monitored over one hundred situations where employees confronted their provocateurs because of uneasy feelings, and the result has always been positive for both parties. Addressing a suspicion at the prevention stage causes a manipulator to be aware his subject will be difficult and he abandons the project. He then spends a great deal of time in his assigned program cooperating in an attempt to prove the employee's suspicion wrong, and in this process, develops habit patterns beneficial to him. When the inmates discover that nonsense has been set aside, they strive to prove to the ex-proposed victim that they can act appropriately. As these practiced, productive actions become habit, they also become part of the inmates' life style. The inmates become proud of their accomplishments and new ways of coping. Said one inmate, "I never worked a day in my life on the streets. In here I learned a trade and was proud of it. When my vacation time came around, I couldn't stand it. So I went back to work. I like it."

In cases where the employee's suspicion is wrong, the same pattern of behavior occurs. Perhaps the best approach monitored by the authors has been the following discourse:

"You are doing things that make me feel uneasy. Nothing wrong at this point, you understand, but I can see where your behavior is subject to misinterpretation. I've granted favors at your request that really shouldn't have been granted, and after discussing this matter with my peers, I've decided both of us should alter our approach to one another and be more professional in our relationship."

In the cited case, the prisoner was known to be a manipulator. The employee was new to corrections. By discussing his feelings with peers, everything was kept in the open. He did not accuse the inmate of dishonest actions, he only indicated the actions of both of them should be altered. His honesty with the prisoner and decision to change his approach generated respect between the two men. The inmate was so impressed, the balance of his prison stay was spent trying to emulate the employee, and he eventually lost the reputation of manipulator.

Games Criminals Play provides patterned information which, when coupled with the gut level feeling, substantiates or negates one's suspicions. Using the approach similar to the discourse example given earlier in this section permits sensible, non-hostile confrontation and stops the process. Prison personnel must always remember the chief purpose of control is recognition and prevention, which is before the fact, not apprehension and punishment, which is after the fact. Employees must apply their positive personality traits—not to foolish games—but to the advancement of their professional selves, the progression of inmate treatment, and the betterment of their detention facility.

Manipulators
at
Large

This text has dealt chiefly with the issue of set-ups as they occur in the prison setting, which—as previously pointed out—is a major problem of many detention facilities. Because the authors have used prisons as their laboratory, one might gain the erroneous impression that set-ups do not occur elsewhere. This would be a serious misunderstanding of the message contained in these pages. Set-ups take place in every facet of society throughout the world. Prisons are simply places where the process is perfected. It is in this cloistered society that the authors were able to view the practice with a much greater accuracy than is possible in an open community. Here they could observe at close range how the adverse manipulation of someone's behavior is conceived, fostered, developed and implemented.

Set-ups are ancient modes of behavior. As far back as history records, individuals or groups of individuals have endeavored to exert influence over others for the purpose of attaining personal gain and/or power. Ever since Cain and Abel, set-ups have always been with us. The process itself never changes, but the techniques of implementing that process have no limit except the individual's ability and imagination.

The authors—in assessing information gleaned by observing set-up behavior, searching prisoner and criminal case files, and acquiring information about set-up victims—have noted several significant factors which form a cycle the reader would do well to remember. The first is: Most criminals possess an almost instinctive ability for, and are extremely well versed in, set-up techniques prior to entering confinement. Second, a number of these convicted felons continue the practice while imprisoned, using institution employees as their victims. Third, set-up techniques are perfected in prison. In this capsule society, the possibility of detection is much greater than in the free world, so these deceptive people must learn to ply their trade with more skill and sophistication. And finally, many of these criminals, upon re-entry into the world outside prison walls, continue to practice a more perfected and subtle style of deception which they acquired during their period of incarceration. However, it should be stressed once again that not all criminals or ex-convicts are manipulators, but rest assured, they all recognize and understand the total set-up process.

THE STREET PSYCHOLOGIST AT WORK

In comparing prison set-ups to those practiced in the community, some interesting procedural variations are brought to light. For example, prison set-ups usually require the use of all fourteen steps described in this text to be suc-

214

cessful. The street set-up artist, on the other hand, may understand all of the steps, but—depending on what is to be gained—quite often only uses a few. The reason? The more people to select from the greater the chance of finding susceptible victims; and, detection of these deceptive practices is more difficult in the open community. However, the reader should be aware that the more valuable the prize, the more set-up steps a deceiver will need to use. Another factor is that set-ups are more prevalent in today's society, because there seems to be an ever increasing number of people who respond to manipulators using the "something for nothing" approach to coercion.

THE "SOMETHING FOR NOTHING" SET-UP APPROACH

This method of deception presupposes that most human beings become somewhat greedy—thus, less cautious or suspicious—when they think they can get something for nothing; that people of little means will respond to the ploy out of necessity; and that, people are easy "marks" or victims. The "something for nothing" set-up approach is a process of creating a condition or situation which makes it difficult for an intended victim to say NO. This is done by having something of value present for a victim to *see* and *touch.* The theory is that if a potential victim can see and touch a much-wanted item, desire for possession is heightened and can overshadow reason. Another factor in this set-up technique is *urgency:* "If you don't respond now, you won't have another chance." And, last but not least is *secrecy:* "This deal is only for you because you're special, but if you tell anyone, the deal is off."

The following two examples—one mild and one serious—show the process in action.

The Chosen Ones
This case involves door-to-door, hard sell salesmanship

which seeks to place a person under obligation by contract using distortion of fact, and the elements just discussed in the "something for nothing" approach.

By relating this situation, the authors are not condemning or placing judgment, but rather are showing the effectiveness of the "something for nothing" theory in sales when combined with "see and touch, urgency, and secrecy." The authors would also like to point out that door-to-door selling is a respected profession, and most salesmen involved in the trade are trustworthy. There are, however, some people in this type of selling whose ethics leave something to be desired.

Using the Test of Limits and/or Fish Testing, this con-wise door-to-door salesman uses the law of averages—the number of people approached in a day—for victim selection. The easy mark is subjected to a well-rehearsed patter that goes something like this:

"Good morning! This is certainly your lucky day! You have been selected as one of three people in your neighborhood to receive, at no cost, this beautiful once-in-a-lifetime product."

He opens his case so the set can be seen and hands one of the prized objects to his proposed victim. The product *is* very nice looking. His patter continues: "Aren't they beautiful?"

"Well . . . ah . . . yes, they are," the victim says, "but no cost . . . ?"

"Absolutely none! . . . except maybe a small shipping and handling charge. But that's something no one can escape, as you well know, my friend."

The victim agrees.

"Your only obligation to my company will be to display this eye-catching set in a prominent place so friends and relatives can see it. You don't have to sell or say anything about our product. You can see how beautiful the workmanship is.

They don't take up much room, and for the value you and your family will receive at no cost, a person would be foolish to be without them. Don't you agree?"

"Well . . . I . . . er . . . guess so, it is a nice set, but I . . ."

The salesman begins speaking without allowing his victim to finish. "You do realize, of course, that your standing in the community has made you eligible to receive this offer. Ordinarily, we only place these sets in the homes of doctors, lawyers, judges, and . . . "

"Gosh, I didn't realize that." The victim seems impressed and continues with: "Well, I do work hard and I try to be fair and honest. . . . "

"I know you do and that's why you were selected to receive this set." The salesman, sensing his timing is right, picks up his case and steps through the doorway while continuing the sales pitch. "But, you really must see the set on a table, shelf, or mantle to appreciate its full beauty!"

Once inside, much time is spent complimenting the condition of the home and exclaiming how the set will be the perfect addition to the room decor. Once a display site has been determined and the salesman is placing his product for inspection, the following admonition is issued: "Oh, I almost forgot, there is one other condition for receiving this set for only shipping and handling plus a small commission for my trouble." This is said quickly and in low tones. "You must promise not to tell your friends and relatives you received this set at no cost other than shipping, handling, and commission. You will do that, won't you?"

"Well . . . yes . . . but I haven't said . . . "

Again, not allowing the statement to be finished, the salesman interrupts: "This set is valued at over $2,500. Our company can't afford to do this except for just a few select people, but I don't really need to tell you that; a person in your position can understand the need for discretion."

217

"Well, I do try to keep my word . . . but . . ."

The set is displayed, and with childlike amazement, the salesman says: "What a beautiful compliment to your home. Just look at that! Aren't they a real part of this room?"

"Yes . . . they do look nice," the victim agrees.

"They belong here at any cost," the salesman insists, "but they're yours for only the commission, handling and shipping. I can't even get a set with that kind of deal for my own home and I'm a salesman for the company! Let me use your table to bring my records up to date, and you can look around the room to get a feeling of where you would like to display them permanently. Hope you don't mind my asking you a few questions. We must have a record of where these sets are placed."

"No, I don't mind . . . The regular cost is over $2,500, you say . . . ?"

The victim likes the set and the salesman and wants to keep the product. The salesman records name, address and other contractual essentials, plus recording his commission at 15% of $2,500 which is actually the full company retail price for the set. He makes the contract extend over a four year period with monthly payments of twelve dollars a month, then says to his victim: "Well, the set is yours. As nice as it looks there, I couldn't take it out of your house if I wanted to. Now to cover these small costs, I'm giving you four years to pay. All you have to do is drop $12 each month in an envelope and send it to us. Nothing could be easier. Oh, one other thing . . . to show my faith in you, I'm leaving this $2,500 product. As a show of your faith in me, could you give me . . . say . . . . . ah . . . five dollars, and just sign here to show you received the set?"

The victim hands over five dollars, then noticing the balance due of $576, hesitates to sign the contract, saying, "It would really be better to wait a month or so until the family financial situation is improved."

"Oh, I'm sorry," the salesman responds, "but this offer expires at midnight tonight, never to be repeated because it costs the company too much. Oh, how terrible. I would hate to see you lose the chance of a life-time, but . . . "

The victim signs.

In cases of this type, it would be difficult to prove the salesman had done anything illegal. However, new truth-in-lending laws provide protection for people who become involved in contracts they wish to be released from. There is a time limit. Persons wishing information on truth-in-lending can usually obtain it from their bank. Anyone in doubt about a business' reputation should check with the Better Business Bureau or local business association.

The Quick Mark

Recently (1980), in a west coast city of average size, authorities reported investigating a set-up involving Social Security pension checks. In this situation, a shrewd manipulator, using The Observation Process, Selection of a Victim, The Support System and Empathy/Sympathy, manages to dupe people out of their income by a ruse called "The Gold Card."

Realizing that almost everyone is acquainted with an older person on Social Security, the manipulator engages people traveling on city buses in conversation and demeans the system for not paying sufficient retirement income. He indicates to his listeners that he can "help the poor souls" get larger checks if he knew how to contact them. In this fashion, he acquires names, addresses, and information about each pensioner's personality and habits. This provides him with a system for victim selection. He then observes his victim's home, gains additional information from people in the neighborhood, then waits for the person to receive and cash his check. Each month he gathers facts on five people in various parts of the city and figures to "hit" the week Social Security checks are issued. The actual set-up is accomplished in the following manner:

Mr. Jones answers his door bell. The caller, a well-dressed, dignified man, introduces himself as Bill Sloan, Social Security field representative. He produces the appropriate credentials. Taking an envelope from his inside coat pocket, which clearly exposes a portion of several twenty dollar bills, he says, "I'm sorry to disturb you, Mr. Jones, but there has been a mistake on your Social Security check. You have been designated a 'Gold Card Holder', but didn't receive your raise. We owe you an apology and some money, and I'm here to rectify the mistake and bring our records up-to-date. May I come in?"

Once Bill is inside, Mr. Jones inquires: "Gold Card Holder? I'm not sure I understand."

"You mean you don't know about the new program? Perhaps I should explain: The Federal government has finally realized something we office workers have been telling them for years—namely, that you people don't receive enough money to live on. The government can't afford to give everyone a raise right off the bat, so the decision was made to make some of our more outstanding citizens Gold Card Holders and increase their pay benefits. You were one of the people selected—and, by the way, your neighbors think quite highly of you—but for some unknown reason, the computer failed to pick up the information, and you did not receive your raise. So, like I said, we owe you some money."

"Gee, that's great." Mr. Jones seems excited.

Taking the money out of the envelope—approximately $200—Bill moves to the kitchen table and displays the money in a fan shape for best exposure, and continues talking. "Before I can turn this money over to you, Mr. Jones, we have a few record-keeping things to do so this mistake won't be repeated next month, and I must have your promise that you

220

will not spend the additional money foolishly. We want this program to be successful."

Mr. Jones seems uncomfortable at the suggestion he might be unwise in spending the additional funds and says quite defensively, "I never spend money foolishly, you can check . . . "

"Oh, I know you don't, Mr. Jones. That's just one of the things we have to ask."

"Oh, I understand." Mr. Jones feels more comfortable knowing he wasn't under that kind of suspicion, and he assures Bill he would never do anything to jeopardize his Gold Card status.

The ploy tells Bill two things: Mr. Jones wants the money badly enough to be hopeful and trusting, and he didn't suspect anything.

"Let's see, now, Mr. Jones, I will need to see your Social Security check, or if you have cashed it, the money you have left together with an itemized list of things you purchased."

Jones takes the money from a jar in the kitchen cupboard and hands it to Bill, then sits down to itemize his earlier expenditures.

Before long Bill looks up from the form he has been working on and says, "I hope you'll forgive me, Mr. Jones, but according to the information requested on this form, I will need to see your Social Security Card, your Driver's License, and a major credit card if you have one."

Jones leaves the room to get the items requested, and when he returns, all the money and his "official" guest have disappeared.

After accomplishing several hundred such set-ups, the silver-tongued rascal was apprehended and sent to jail.

The victim in this case might have avoided the loss of his money if he had followed a few simple rules:

1. To avoid a you/me situation, never admit a stranger into your home.
2. Keep everything in the open: ask the stranger to wait at the door for a moment. Call the Social Security Office and verify his employment and whether or not a "Gold Card Program" exists. If these things cannot be verified, call the police.
3. Realize that legitimate businesses rarely, if ever, do cash transactions at the door. Bureaucracies never do. You have to go to them.
4. Never conduct cash business requiring large sums of money at your door.

THE PIGEON SET-UP APPROACH

The term pigeon usually denotes a swindle. Here the Observation Process and establishing a You/Me situation and the We/They Syndrome are of prime importance. The manipulator must have advance knowledge of his subject if the swindle is to be successful, because he must be sure that conditions exist which would make his victim susceptible to manipulation. In the case that follows a hate situation which stemmed from one person's desire to outdo the other becomes a lever causing the loss of a fairly substantial amount of money.

Clint and his brother Jack became partners in a construction business, but found they couldn't get along with each other. A split occurred and each became the other's competitor. The division of funds caused each to face financial problems. Previously, they could jointly buy or rent heavy equipment to complete a construction job; separately, each had to forego some of the better income-producing contracts. Each man placed such a heavy emphasis on one-up-manship that

222

a hatred had developed between them. This became the topic of conversation in construction circles.

Bob, a construction worker, kept the fires of hatred burning between the two by transferring information of questionable validity, first to Clint, then to Jack. Because of their dislike for one another, neither brother suspected Bob as being anything other than a friend. A road job was coming up that both Clint and Jack wanted, but it required a piece of equipment neither man had. One day Bob approached Jack and said, "I saw Clint the other day and it looks like he's going to get that road job."

Jack was furious over the news and, in a fit of anger, stated, "No way can he get that job. He doesn't own a road grader and there's none around to rent. I know, I've checked it out!"

"O.K., if you say so," Bob shrugged his shoulders and started to leave.

Jack stopped him saying, "Now hold on, damn it. Do you know something I don't know?"

"Only that a friend of mine has a grader and promised to sell it to Clint for only $15,000. Clint is hocking his business to get the machine.

"Damn!" Jack's anger made his face turn red.

Unknown to Jack, Bob had told the same story to Clint, who responded to the news of his brother's good fortune in much the same manner.

The following day, Bob told Jack he had spoken with the owner of the grader and could arrange a quick sneak sale if Jack could raise two thousand dollars more than Clint. "We'll buy it right out from under Clint's nose," Bob said with a chuckle.

Jack's eyes lit up. "Do you think that's possible?" His voice was like a mischievous little kid.

"Sure, he'll go for it," Bob assured him. "If we can

dangle an extra two thousand under my friend's nose, he'd be a fool not to take it."

"We'll do it, Bob! When can I see the grader?"

Bob took him to a lot on the outskirts of town where the machine was parked, just as he had done to Clint the evening prior. The road knife was in perfect condition. A real "once-in-a-lifetime" buy.

On their return to Jack's office, Bob warned, "if we do this, my friend will have to get out of town fast, because when Clint finds out, he'll kill the guy. You'll have to pick the thing up in a special way, O.K.?"

"I don't care how you do it, Bob, just do it!"

"O.K., here's the way my friend wants to make the transfer. Clint is supposed to pick the grader up at noon on Saturday. I'll have the keys and the owership papers to close the deal. But, here's the most important part: you can't pick the grader up until exactly 8:00 p.m. on Friday night. My friend wants to move the thing after dark so the neighbors won't see who's driving. He doesn't want to run the risk of somebody calling Clint before he gets away."

Jack agreed. He was elated over the prospect of putting one over on Clint. He could hardly wait. He told Bob, "I wish I could see the expression on Clint's face when he finds out I own the grader."

At 1.00 p.m. on Friday, Jack gave Bob $17,000, signed the papers, and received a set of keys.

At 8:00 p.m. that evening, Jack and Clint met face to face at the lot. The grader was gone. Bob, who was $34,000 richer, was gone. But at least the two brothers came away with something—each owned his own set of keys.

THE FLESH PEDDLER SET-UP PROGRAM

Perhaps the saddest and most frightening of all set-ups are those where teen-age boys and girls—mostly run-aways and hitchhikers—are befriended by adults who systematically convert them into thieves and/or prostitutes. It has been estimated that over a million and a half youngsters fall prey to these people every year.

This type of manipulation consists of finding children who are alone and hungry. Flesh peddlers, under the guise of helpfulness, provide them with food, lodging, and spending money. After a short period of time, they demand what the children have spent be returned. Naturally, the children are unable to pay, so beatings take place. Many are raped, forced into drug addiction to make them submissive, then under a threat of death, they are sent to rob, steal, or solicit on the streets.

IT CAN'T HAPPEN TO ME

There are hundreds, perhaps thousands, of set-up variations being used in communities all over the world, every day. The authors have discussed a few in this chapter to give the reader a more graphic exposure, but these illustrate only a minute tip of the iceberg.

Almost everyone has a friend or knows someone who has been the victim of a set-up. This means a tremendous number of people have been affected by the process. Set-ups are one of the most common forms of crime. Every year, people lose millions of dollars to set-up practitioners. Every year, millions of people are projected into some type of serious life-disrupting turmoil when victimized by this process and, every year thousands of people die for refusing some kind of set-up demands. Yet, people still say, "It can't happen to me!"

The idea, "It can't happen to me!" is a widely practiced attitude in the United States, and possibly throughout the world. Criminals rely upon the public's general acceptance of this idea of passivity and self-confidence. It confirms that most people are not much concerned about this type of criminal activity; that criminals can ply their trade without a great deal of outside intervention; and that because this idea is so widely voiced, they are likely to be in business for a long time to come. Everyone should know, understand, be able to detect, recognize, and prevent his or her own victimization and the victimization of others by being aware of Games Criminals Play and Games Manipulators Play. It is to this end that this book was written, and it will have served its purpose if one life is saved, one home made more secure, or one child spared from physical and mental degradation. And, everyone should realize that without the slightest doubt, IT CAN HAPPEN TO YOU.

About
the
Authors

≈≈

Bud Allen and Diana Bosta created this unique treatise in the hope that it would aid the relationships of all people involved in the correctional process. Lieutenant Allen contributed his many years of experience in corrections as an officer, sergeant, counselor, lieutenant and assistant academy director. He is a social scientist who received his education from the University of California and his graduate degree from the University of San Francisco. Besides his Community College credential, he holds credentials in 27 specialized fields of criminal justice. He is a trained investigator, rangemaster and martial arts specialist. He has served as consultant to the California prisons, a number of colleges, The Department of Fish and Game, probation departments, and police and corrections training academies.

Mrs. Bosta contributed her non-custody prison teaching experience. She is an education consultant and reading specialist who has dealt with special people throughout her entire career. Her aim in corrections is to cause the lesser-desired life styles to fade out while ushering in a more appropriate life orientation for the recalcitrant individual. She received her education from the University of Michigan and her graduate degree from the University of Nevada. She holds a Community College credential and has had extensive training in the area of criminal justice. She has been a reading consultant in California, Nevada and Oregon.

Both authors have faced the set-up process many times, but because they can recognize coercion in its infancy, they prevent the situation from progressing. They are partners in a consulting firm—DiAllen Associates—and promote making detention and correction facilities a better place for employees to work and for inmates to live. Both reside in California.